Nell's

Story

Nell's Story

A Woman from Eagle River

by
Nell Peters
with
Robert Peters

The University of Wisconsin Press

A North Coast Book

The University of Wisconsin Press
114 North Murray Street
Madison, Wisconsin 53715

3 Henrietta Street
London WC2E 8LU, England

Copyright © 1995
The Board of Regents of the University of Wisconsin System

1   3   5   4   2

Library of Congress Cataloging-in-Publication Data
Peters, Nell, 1932–
Nell's story: a woman from eagle river
Nell Peters and Robert Peters.
172 pp.   cm.
"North Coast book."
ISBN 0-299-14470-4 (cloth)
1. Peters, Nell, 1932–   2. Wisconsin—Biography.
3. Women—Wisconsin— Biography. 4. Wisconsin—Social life and customs.
I. Peters, Robert, 1924–   . II. Title.
CT275.P582A3   1995
997.5'04'092—dc20
[B]   94-24164

For our Parents Sam and Dorothy Peters
For our sisters Marjorie Mayo and Jane Zuidmulder
and
For Mike, David, and Martin, Marilyn, Shannon,
and Gus, and for Dan, David, Benji, Ericka, Nicole, Terra,
and Brittany
and for Paul Trachtenberg who assisted us with
our numerous writings and rewritings

Contents

Prefatory Note

Robert Peters

I INVITED my sister Nell to write the story of her life as a child, adolescent, WAC, wife, mother, American Legion Post commandant, and survivor. She obliged, scribbling onto yellow legal pads during the icy Wisconsin winter months when her perpetual garage sale was closed. After reading her first fifty pages, I realized that she had an engrossing, rare, and moving story. I saw, too, that despite her lack of a formal education, she has always read much, and has a larger vocabulary than one would expect from a woman growing up without advantages. Moreover, her colorful speech has everywhere heightened this memoir.

Pressed by other writing deadlines, I postponed our book until the spring of 1991 when friend and poet Paul Trachtenberg and I drove from southern California to Wisconsin, where we rented a cabin on Duck Lake, on the famous Chain of Lakes. Mornings on our dewy lawn, hungry robins, newly arrived from their migration, feasted on enormous angleworms. Only in the final days did the mosquitos for which the Northland is famous arrive in force.

Nell proved an ideal subject, for she was anxious to tell her story, warts and all. We often wrote for five and six hours at a stretch, drinking coffee and eating doughnuts, and fried pike, perch, crappies, and bass, courtesy of Nell's sons Gus and Marty, her grandson Danny, and her son-in-law Dan. With my computer up, and with her manuscript in view, I wrote, interweaving her fresh memories with old ones. For both of us the experience was often painful, and, for Nell, harrowing, particularly when her struggle to raise her illegitimate twin sons and the impact of that struggle on our parents surfaced. To her credit there was nothing she would not confront, and with amazing clarity and honesty. We both came to understand one another as brother and sister in ways we never hitherto had—and this became one of the subtexts of the book. And our joy in the pleasures of that isolated life, and in our family, and particularly in that incredible setting with its hundreds of glaciated lakes, forests, and flora and fauna are all celebratory. Our book contains much humor throughout. We feel that our collaboration is unique. Nell, who recently turned sixty-two, hopes to inspire other women facing thwarted lives.

In November, 1992, Nell flew to my home in California where with Paul Trachtenberg's critical assistance, she read the entire manuscript aloud, checking on the authenticity. I wanted to be absolutely sure that my penchant for literary flourishes never obtruded. Encouraged by readings of the University of Wisconsin Press staff, and particularly by an astute reading of the manuscript by Rosalie M. Robertson (which helped me rethink the structure), I began yet another revision this past November. Also, the warm support of Professor Dale Bauer, English Department, University of Wisconsin—Madison, has been critical.

We are grateful to Nell's children Marilyn, Shannon, August, and Martin for their enthusiasm. Also, our sisters Marge and Jane have been supportive, though there have been moments when we were sure they have felt misused and misread. We apologize, and express our thanks and love for their patience.

Our dedication of *Nell's Story* to our parents Sam and Dorothy Peters is a small token, after all these years, of the still vibrant love we hold for them. Once the book is published and we place a copy of it face down on their graves in the Eagle River Cemetery, through some mysterious osmosis, they may perhaps know of and approve our effort.

Robert Peters
Huntington Beach, California
22 January 1994

Nell's
Story

Well, Here We Go

"SHADOW! DAMN YOU! Why do you shit right where I walk! If you dig another hole by the door I'll saw your front legs off."

This dog will kill me. I should have gotten a short-hair, like Mom's little wiener dog. And this morning, of all mornings, when I want to sit here in the sun, tend my garage sale, and make a few bucks. There, I've scraped the poop off my heels. Shadow's big and shaggy with a head like a wolf's and with rich fur, almost black, especially around her neck and chest. She poops too much. There's nothing wrong with her crap—not runny—yet she drops it where I don't see it, so that I end up with smeared shoes. I should take her to a vet; but a vet costs as much as a doctor. Shadow's spayed—I think that's the word. Owned her since she was a pup, and I've trained her like I have my six kids: if they don't mind me, I scream.

The command Shadow obeys best is "Shadow, lay down!" shouted with all the lung power I can muster. She licks my hand and cowers. Beat 'em and they come slinkin' back wagging their tails. They've got bad memories and think you love 'em right after you've beaten 'em. Well, I don't want to get too deep, for I know that I'm talking about my kids. I raised them with one hand holding an ice cream bar, the other a belt. Though I like scaring kids and dogs (and stupid men), I'm a softie, and enjoy cuddling kids—always have and always will. Yet, these critters, kids and dogs, love me no matter how I rant and carry on. I vow I'll change, but what I am I am. You get, as Tammy Wynette says, just what you see. A woman alone needs a dog, and if Shadow upsets the neighbors with her barking, so what: nobody will bring his ass to my door uninvited as long as Shadow's here. I sleep in peace, with no prowlers flipping through to my bedroom. I never sleep nude; even in summer I wear a flannel nightie with pink bows at the throat

3

covered with cute girls in sunbonnets. I also wear panties, memories of younger days when I was sexier.

Bob, you said you wanted this story, warts and all, and, sure, I won't pretend that some of this stuff is hard to recollect. I might embarrass my kids and grandkids. But, Christ, it's my life, right? Maybe I can inspire some woman out there as lost as I was who has to struggle putting food on her table, finding clothes for her kids, and hoping for some love along the way. While social programs now help, there are lots of women out there as numerous as pimples on a wart hog, suffering alone, usually with snotty kids clinging to their knees, struggling as I did, or even worse. These women should like my story.

Well, I've waited for over an hour, seated in this twisted old lawn chair, for customers. Most buyers are a mix of needy locals and flushed tourists slumming to keep from being so bored. I like customers I'm comfortable with, and that don't include snotty tourists looking down their noses at me. Sure, everybody says that this part of Wisconsin, as far north as you can get without hitting Upper Michigan, is beautiful, filled as it is with fir trees and pure glaciated lakes. The tourists flock here to hunt, fish, and enjoy the scenery. Sure, we have miserable cold, wet, summers. The Muskie Capital of the World! You've seen those posters. Now we're the "Snowmobile Capital of the USA." And on we go.

Glad you're here, Bob, to listen to my ramblings. I'll make notes, too, this winter when I've got free time, to go along with the ones you're making now. When you get back to California send me a bunch of those big yellow pads with lines. I'll fill 'em, I promise. There may be a good story in my crazy life.

I wish I had a bigger garage. Things tumble out the door of this single-car one: junky tables, chairs, lamps; collector-item high-line-wire insulators, both green and white, each quite heavy. They make great paper weights, or set them up on a hostess bar in your den, conversation pieces when your guests get smashed. Most of those shelves are on chains to be lowered when I close up shop for the winter, usually right after deer season, near Thanksgiving. Some of the income helps the Disabled American Veterans. I've sold boats, tools, and even cars on commission. Most of my customers, though, are poor like me, and find living in this northern resort area, popular with fishing and snow-mobile nuts, hard. While prices for staples fall some during off-season months, they soar when tourists from Milwaukee, Chicago, and points south, flock here. The area has tons of summer homes for the rich and camps for their high-falutin' kids escaping hot, muggy cities. Remember how Dad never got around to finishing the inside of our family house? He left the studs bare so that through the knotholes you could see the snowdrifts pile. And the flimsy tarpaper roof was so skinny the nails holding it to the scrap-lumber boards stuck through, collected teats of ice overnight, and then dripped in our faces as we lay in our beds, waiting for the house to warm up. I don't know how we survived, do you? Yet, I agree, it was a good life in lots of ways. We didn't know any more; although, as you say, once we started high school in town, we knew houses were better-built, and the furniture wasn't somebody else's discards. I've never felt apologetic for our life, and I'm sure you haven't either.

I need my customers not only for the DAV but for supplementing my disability from Social Security and the Veterans' Administration. Right now the latter are hassling me, saying they've overpaid my benefits. How can I live on $350 a month? In 1980 my spine fused and my shitty job soldering wires to the bottoms of batteries, at the local electric company, stopped. Sickening. At age forty-eight I was on the sidelines. No one would hire a back problem, and I had kids to raise. My withering leg happened because of the pinched nerve in my back. I don't have much control over those flabby muscles, and I've lost my dream of buying a big old used Harley Davidson and, wearing leather and chains, sailing across the country to California and finding true love and happiness at last with like-minded biker gals.

After the injury my options were few. I'd work at home. I was always good at fixing vacuum cleaners, bicycles, toasters, stereos, and TVs. Had a real knack for it, probably got it from Pa. I love people's discards, which I take apart, and make run again. So far this year I've sold three repaired vacuums. When word gets out that I do good work, customers come. Poor ones, again, who can't afford to junk their stuff when it quits working. Ironic that the time I use repairing items hardly pays, so I'm never above the poverty line. Pa's philosophy of life was that poor folks have to fix their own things. Any car, tool, boat, churn, or ironing board gone bad you just can't toss out, since there's no money for a new one. When Pa finally bought me a used bike, one in miserable shape, he had me take it apart and re-assemble it.

My garage-sale business grew straight from my repair work. If I was going to fix other people's junk, I might as well collect it, get it working again, and sell it. I've always been hooked on machines, and I'm proud of my physical strength (some say that my shoulders are as broad as Dad's) and I have always liked work. House-cleaning and "women's activities" bore me, as do wearing frocks, pumps, and frilly aprons. I'd much rather be out sopping up car-oil than baking crumb-top apple pies. I guess I'll always feel this way; although, over the years, raising six kids has forced me into the kitchen, usually hit-or-miss, and I can, believe it or not, make a great raisin pie. And my spaghetti, in a hot venison sauce, is the best.

My inventory grows when I visit other garage sales, offering them chicken feed to buy out what's not sold. I offer half what the owners ask. On a rating of ten, with a ten going to the garage sale with the best junk, mine probably rates a two or three, although I make up for it by charging cheap and by displaying my wares to look good, washing them and checking to be sure they work. My only advertising is that pair of signs I painted and stake in front of my house. When I see Mr. and Mrs. Money Bags–Fancy Car drive up I jack up prices; half the fun is haggling. When I come down, they're pleased, so they go off happy—which makes for good business. When I see a poor customer, I'll donate items to them on behalf of the DAV, which looks good for our organization. Public Good Will, I call it.

How you set up stuff matters a lot: pictures hung at eye level in the garage get attention. Just below, I place knickknacks and plastic flowers. Prospective buyers browse and purchase. Take a look there, behind me. See that clock made from lacquered pine? I'm so proud of it. There are Jim Beam decanters, a picture of a sailing ship in a big storm, Avon perfume bottles shaped like cars, presidents, capitol buildings, and guns. There's holiday stuff—ceramic turkey gobblers, Easter baskets, plastic Santas and sleighs, and there's even a Christmas tree with all the lights. Paperback books sell good, especially in summer when it rains and tourists can't go out on the lakes. Until recently there wasn't a single book store in town.

While my garage sales don't make me rich, they pay my taxes and help buy the cigarettes I won't stop smoking. Yes, I know, you're always on my case about them, and I want to quit . . . you know how it is. Best of all, the sales make me feel I'm a contributing member of society. But I want to lure more stuff to my garage for free. With the town dump closed now, people have a hard time getting rid of junk. That's where I come in, and where the Disabled American Vets organization comes in. Contributions to the DAV are all gratuitous. Like I said earlier, for cleaning, repairing, and displaying goods for sale, I'm entitled to a percentage. What doesn't sell in the summer is mine, and I start collecting all over in the spring. Since my withered leg keeps me close to home, I'm always available.

I am proud of my DAV and American Legion ties. In fact, over the past seventeen years I've been commander, adjutant, and finance officer. I've organized Memorial Day, Fourth of July, and Veterans' Day events, including marches to the local cemetery and festivities by the river that cuts through the town where Boy Scouts and Girl Scouts toss poppies and other war memorial flowers. When I don my jaunty blue uniform cap and my Frederick J. Walsh Post blazer, I feel proud honoring those who gave their lives so that the rest of us can be safe in our beds. As I stand at attention with fellow vets, I recall those men (and women) who sacrificed so much. How easily we forget. Some merchants either refuse contributions or fail to display the flag. We write letters to the local paper, naming names, which does some good, but not enough. There's never been a boycott of such businesses.

Currently I am an adjutant for the DAV, and last year was commander. An experience I much enjoy is what we call King's Day, where we adopt a crippled older veteran who is in his final years at the veterans' home in King, Wisconsin. We have a barbecue, card-playing, and boat rides. Because of my roles with the DAV and the Legion, I often wear a mixed uniform. How did I become a vet? I signed on with the WACs, in the American Women's Army Corps, in 1951.

Though my stint in the WACs was a horrible seven months, I've always needed to be useful to my country. Any person who draws on society must put something back for the next guy. It's like crossing a desert where you're about to die of thirst, and you find a goat-skin full of sweet water. You don't drink it all, and once you've drunk, you fill the skin again at the next oasis, for another thirsty traveller.

Damn, this is a slow day, and like so many beautiful mornings here, by 10 o'clock, rain clouds belly up like big sheep and drop the temperature ten or fifteen degrees. You can see the pine trees shiver. We get tornados from plunges in barometric pressure, from the collisions of currents fighting the jet streams flying over the hundreds of lakes, large and small, which cover this region, and from the storm clouds winging down from Canada, some fifty miles as the crow flies. But you know all about this. Remember, Bob, that July afternoon when we stood on the hill near the house and we watched the black funnel driving towards us, hitting first across Minnow Lake by Ewald's farm? We clustered in the living room around Dad who said we'd be safe; if we had to he'd pop up the root cellar door and we'd scurry down there. I've never been so scared as I was when that twister roared over the house and lightning and thunder flashed and exploded. Seems like we had one such episode every summer, which didn't make them any less scary.

Wait! There's a Ford pick-up with a rusted body and cancerous muffler. Those two Indian women bought an old brown couch last week. Are they returning the damn thing? Have they come for the table and chairs they didn't have the money to pay for? It's the second of the month; welfare checks were in the mail yesterday.

The younger woman's climbing out. She's the short one with moles like blueberries on her cheeks. Her purple sweat pants are too tight for her belly, and that white T-shirt with "Budweiser" across the front and "Corner Bar, Crandon, Wisconsin" on the back sure don't leave much to the imagination. So, Bob, you sit tight. I'll go deal with them.

"Hi, was the couch OK?"

"Sure. The kids is jumpin' all over it, and so are the dogs. I need another one. Did one come in?"

"No, but I still have the overstuffed chairs and the table. Do you want those now?"

"Take a look, Mom." An aged woman, toothless, with parched purple skin, her hair in black plaits, comes over.

"Twenty dollars for all three," I say, "which is just about what I paid for them. A bargain. Take a look at the legs—they'll take a bunch of abuse."

While the daughter and I were loading the furniture into the truck, the old squaw meandered to the rear of the garage and picked up a stuffed teddy bear, a fifty-cent item. She touched the animal to her cheek, then put it back down.

She smiled.

"Would you like that?" I ask. "It's a present. Free."

I hand it to her.

She thanks me, bows, and returns to the truck.

Since they paid me with a ten-dollar bill, a fiver, and an assortment of quarters, I put the bills in my pocket, and the change into a can I keep for coins. Rain threatens. Seeing the old squaw leads me to recall when Mom died thirteen years ago, aged seventy-four, with severely hardened arteries and internal bleeding. How tough her life was! But, she was a survivor, as I am—she taught me that; and nothing makes this clearer than her life of poverty, illness, and all the babies. Among her seven pregnancies (including two miscarriages), I was number four. I still choke up thinking how warm her neck was when we'd kiss her.

1

Kerosene Lamps, Birth, and Childhood

—⊙⊙⊙—

1932

—⊙⊙⊙—

YOU WERE only seven, Bob, on January 8, 1932. There was a heavy snowstorm. The sky, cold steel, was chilled with swirling snowflakes. Here was the picture: a burly man on skis, wearing gum-soled boots, bib overalls, a plaid mackinaw jacket reaching to his knees, and brown knit cap, with globs of hoarfrost all over his face, bearing his bundled wife in his arms, struggled through drifts filling up his tracks as soon as he'd cut them. He passed stands of spruce, white birch, pine, and dormant sumac, some still bearing red fruit, food for sparrows and chickadees.

The man hunched, almost losing his balance when a ski struck some stump or tree root. Dorothy Peters, wrapped in a wool blanket, her feet stuffed into buckled overshoes, wearing earmuffs and cap, though warm, was frightened. The birth waters for her fourth child had broken and the pains, she guessed, were about two minutes apart. In all that snow, no car could have made it to town. The Model-T Ford wouldn't have gotten through the front yard. No snow plows would appear that day, not until the snow stopped.

The trip in the storm took Dad nearly an hour, so he and Mom told me. They left you at home with Marge and Everett, who were six and four. Dad's destination? He was headed for his brother's, where Geshom's wife Kate would help Mom while Dad borrowed a horse to ride to town for the doctor. There was no guarantee, of course, he'd find Doc Oldfield at home. They'd have a snow plow come out ahead so that Doc could get through.

Aunt Kate was a portly French Canadian who believed in magic.

10

Mom said that she used no hocus pocus this time, but made her comfortable in her bed, spooned chicken soup and tea, and waited. She sent her daughter Florence to watch you kids. When the doctor arrived, Mom's pains were at one-minute intervals. Dr. Barney Oldfield, a cigar-smoking, gruff GP, the town's surgeon, hardly had time to get his coat off and his hands washed before he saw the future Me, all red-haired, ready to burst from Mom's womb.

Bare-handed, so Mom said, he yanked me out. "It's a girl." His voice, Mom reported, was anxious. You never knew with "country births." The nearest hospital, Catholic St. Mary's, was twenty-three miles away, in Rhinelander.

Kate brought towels, and after the doctor cleaned me and dropped nitrate in my eyes, he put me in Mom's arms. "I'm calling her Nellie Emma," Dorothy announced.

"OK by me," Doc said "But aren't those old-fashioned?"

"Nellie's my favorite sister," Dorothy explained. "She's in Kansas now, but she lived with us when Bob was born, and she went to high school in Eagle River. Emma was my mother's name, Emma Haverland Keck."

"I'll always call her Cocoa," Doc said, "which is what I'd like to drink right now, Kate, as hot as you can make it."

Mom and I stayed with my uncle and aunt for three days, until the road was plowed, when Dad took us home. Since I was born in my aunt's bed, she felt bonded, our paths later crossing tragically. She complained that Uncle Pete liked me more than he did his own kids. He'd spend hours rocking me in an old cherry rocker, singing along while wax cylinder records played on a wind-up phonograph. His favorite was "Barney Google": *Barney Google, with the googly-googly eyes. . . .*" I still remember those old records, how each one fit snug inside a cardboard cylinder lined with sheepskin, and how the skin smelled. Uncle Pete never let anyone but him play the records.

My namesake aunt, Aunt Nell, until her death, in Radium, Kansas, in 1983, often phoned: "Hello, Nell? This is Nell." I never met Grandma Emma Haverland Keck, although you, Bob, as a child of three, visited her in Ellsworth, Kansas. I've always liked that picture of you clad in overalls, in the middle of her flock of Plymouth Rock hens, throwing a tantrum. Grandma has you by the hand—but she's not having any luck quieting you down.

The House That Dad Built
—⟨⟨⟨⟩⟩⟩—

OUR OLD HOUSE, twenty feet square, was built by Dad's father Richard from pine and cedar logs dragged from the swamps with a horse and stone-boat, which he peeled and stood one beside the other, interlocking the corners with deft axe strokes, further securing them by wooden dowels rather than nails. Spaces between the logs he chinked with moss and smeared over with thick plaster. The low roof, to stop snow build-up and collapse, formed a V. Smaller logs and slabs of third-grade lumber, covered with tarpaper, formed the roof. A floor was made of more scrap culled from the local Wisconsin Michigan sawmill. Eventually, we bought cheap linoleum, and Mom hooked rugs from old dresses, shirts, and trousers. In the middle of the cozy living room was a trap door complete with ring and crude wooden ladder down which you climbed to an earthen root cellar where summer produce—potatoes, cabbage, carrots, and an assortment of canned wild fruit and vegetables were kept. For more warmth and security, the house windows were small, with neat curtains Mom made from bleached flour sacks. She'd brought along a treadle sewing machine on her wedding trip from North Dakota, and she kept it all her life, even after she went electric.

A second room half the size of the first was added on shortly after Mom and Dad married, in the summer of 1923. Dad's dad then returned to Indiana with his German mistress Pearl, who was with him until he died in 1931.

The only other building on the property was a lean-to of logs built for chickens, raised some four feet off the ground to be safe from skunks and weasels. It was covered with chicken-wire and had a drop door for use in winter. Inside were nesting boxes filled with straw.

When I was three, in 1935, we moved half a mile away to a forty-acre parcel Dad bought on the installment plan from President Roosevelt's Home Owner's Loan Corporation program, designed to give needy families small farms. Total cost: $350 to be paid off in monthly installments of thirty dollars. During this time, Dad worked forty-hour weeks building roads for Roosevelt's Works Project Administration. His pay was ninety dollars per month plus welfare groceries. The land, less swampy than the old place, bordered on Mud Minnow Lake, which was encircled by cranberry bogs and teemed with fingerling perch. The house itself stood on a birch knoll a hundred yards from the main gravel road and the mailbox.

The Broken Arm: 1938

"WELL, what's happened to her?" Doc Flannery, the retired Army doctor with the William Powell mustache, asked Dad.

We'd driven in over ice, after I fell off my chair and damaged my arm—how bad we didn't know. Shortly after 6 p.m. (Dad was in the barn milking), I was in my high chair—the tray had been lifted off. You'd removed the tray so that I could get closer to you kids at the table doing homework by kerosene lamp. I was five years old. You, Bob, had your history book open to a picture of Roman soldiers fighting some Greeks. You liked those old times, and even gave me a picture book of stories about their gods for Christmas. I liked the Apple of Discord story. Those bodies were draped in see-through gauze, and their wrists were so feminine. They sprang right off the page, dancing, craving for that golden apple. I was in love with all of them. When you started to explain a picture of Zeus's cupbearer, my chair slipped back, tumbling me to the linoleum.

Stunned, hurt, I knew something awful had happened. You got Dad from the barn. On the way to town I sat on your lap. Our regular doctor was out, so we roused Dr. Flannery, who had recently moved here from Milwaukee for the fishing.

"Well," Flannery said, bending over the arm. "It could be worse. It's a sprain. Just put hot, wet towels on it. Have them so hot she can barely stand it." Like most people, we saw doctors as gods.

Home again, Marge and Everett made me feel the accident was my fault. Mom had sympathy. Because of the swelling, Dad sat up with me all night applying heat. The pain ran from my elbow right up to the top of my skull. Finally, two days later, with the swelling bigger than ever, we saw Dr. Oldfield.

"This is a god-damned mess," Dr. Barney shouted, once Miss Berry put us in his examining room. "Heat's the worst thing, Sam. This arm's fractured."

He tried to bend the arm. "We'll use some ether," he said. "Then she won't feel what I'm doing."

When I came out of the ether, Dr. Barney laughed: "Coco, you cussed a blue streak, worthy of a mule-skinner. I didn't know you knew those words." He paused. "You'll be stiff for awhile." Because the tissue was already knit he wouldn't rebreak the bone. As long as I could wiggle the arm, it was best not to risk more damage.

"She'll have a bump," he said. "It won't keep her from attracting a good man someday."

All my life I looked double-jointed, with bone spurs. Ten years ago, I fell on ice, rebroke the arm, and, finally, had it properly reset. That experience, so young, taught me to take pain without too much flinching. And don't jump to conclusions: I hate pain. People have different levels of tolerance. I've chopped an index finger open to the bone and had it sewn back up without Novocain. When my brother-in-law Bob Kauth was home on leave, I jumped on his back and his judo chop sent me flying against his suitcase where I slashed my chin on a hasp. Doc Barney pushed the gaping meat together and, without pain killer, used cat gut or whatever. I survived. My stand on pain? You can't avoid it, and you'll get big doses before you die. Whoever said life was sweet?

The Best Boy Dad Ever Had

DAD LOVED ME more than Mom did. Of a family of six I was, so Aunt Kate said, the least wanted. As an "accident" I should have run down Mom's leg when Dad spurted the seed.

Looking back after nearly sixty years, I can see why Mom wished I wasn't born. Married at seventeen, snatched from a large North Dakota family, badly educated (she dropped out after one year in a prairie high school), aware of nothing ahead but being a housewife, she agreed to marry the good-looking farm worker on her dad's threshing crew. When he was four, Sam Peters's own mother, sick with diphtheria and a split appendix, lay in a sod house near Gary, Indiana, dying. Only Sam was with her when she died. Raised by a sister Caroline until the age of seven or eight, Dad spent his adolescence alone. His dad scavenged coal from worn-out mines, boozed, and chased whores. Mom was more of a mother to Dad than a wife.

An aunt in Everett, Washington, Leora Willard, now gone, did send us that story on Dad. I keep it right here in this bag of papers. It's a treasure, and tells us what Pa was like as a kid: He, his sister Calley (Caroline), and his father Richard visited with Leora and her family in North Dakota, c. 1909, when Dad was seven. They called him "Sammy." He stayed with Leora and briefly went to school. "Always," Leora writes, "when he came he was dirty, ragged, and poorly clothed, and Mother always washed, mended, and replenished his worn-out clothing for him while there, and when he went home." When Calley brought her new husband Enoch Samuelson to visit, "Sammy ran and crawled beneath Mother's bed, making a barking dog's noise. It took a bit of coaxing to get him to come out to her. He was rather timid among strangers."

She also mentions our grandfather, Dad's dad Richard. He had opened up a private mine in the side of a hill. Not too many customers came, though, for there was a bigger mine nearby at Avoca. "Uncle Dick surely had to work hard, for back then they had no such tools as they do now. Just a pick and shovel, and maybe a sledge hammer. Even grubbing a scant living from his mine was hard. And I am sorry to say that he was a fat person and not too ambitious to start with. I can see his loneliness and sorrow when he lost his companion. He had much to be sorrowful about."

When Mom was barely twenty, without any other women to talk to, she was saddled with two tots. Her nearest relation was Aunt Kate. Kate was always snotty to Mom because she (Kate) wanted Dad to marry her oldest daughter Annie. Annie was what you'd call a "ball buster." She drove men off. A sailor she married made yearly visits from Argentina where he lived, keeping himself far away from her nagging. And she had a big nose and wore her hair in a shag so messy it looked as if she'd done it herself by feel, without a mirror. Kate stirred up trouble between my folks, whispering stuff to Dad that would make him jealous of Mom. She gave Mom old French-Canadian folk remedies for miscarriages. Pregnant again, Mom did not want a new child any more than she'd wanted me. Kate fed her a mix of kerosene laced with pig grease and pepper. The new child, Everett, had a mild epilepsy which Mom always blamed herself for. She'd tried every way she could to jar the foetus loose. Nothing worked.

Right off, I was Dad's "boy." I ached for him to come home from town where he worked in a garage. I liked his crankcase oil and grease stink. Unlike Mom, I never hated the engine dirt ground into his hands and face. Whenever I got sick, Dad gave me love. When he caught chicken pox from me, he really suffered. Mom said the pox had "gone down" on him. Not only might he be "sterile," he could even die. I was scared. On the front door, the County Nurse tacked a sign "Contagious Family." We were "quarantined." I felt like we had the plague, and was scared of what the school kids would say. Fortunately, Dad recovered.

Why was I so close to Dad? Are most girls that way with their pas? You, Bob, were always closer to Mom. You really never knew that I wasn't much loved, that I hung in the background without being either real happy or real sad. Like, I early caught on: don't ask too much from life, and you won't get hurt. I had red hair, was chubby, and had more freckles than a speckled goose egg. Also, I preferred cows and chickens and fields and woods to people and stuffy houses. Yes, there was one more stigma (I think that's the word): a birthmark pig about two inches long raced over my belly. It was a *pig*, no matter which way you squinted. I could make him fat or skinny according to how I pinched myself. I sure didn't need that curse—I felt I'd been stamped the way the government stamps meat: "U.S. Government Dis-approved." The other kids made up a song they sang when I was cross, and often when I was coming out of a hard nap: "Nelly, Nelly, Stick Stick Stelly, has an ache in her big fat belly." Another song was: "Nellie's got freckles a million score. They're as big as nickels but she still wants more." Mom said I was a family "throwback," to what I don't know. To some cave woman who got hit with a bowl of hot mastodon grease? And Mom said she'd pickled pig's feet the fall she was carrying me. Crazy, but my Uncle Pete had a piglet on his arm, and two of my kids have them. I liked Uncle Pete a lot, though he scared me.

Our sister Marge was born beautiful. She even won a contest at a prom, dressed as a matador. I remember how left out I felt when I sniffed her gardenia corsage, just before she went out the door to meet Hiram Ewald, who was driving her to the dance in his Model-A Ford. Afterwards, she gave me the flower, and, though it turned brown, I kept it with other treasures in a cardboard box under my bed.

But I want this clear; I never felt too sorry for myself then or now. I learned early that if you take the teasing, your tormentors will stop. Dad's love helped, and when I was outside following him around chopping trees, tending to crops and animals, I had no chains. In fact, today, I can even be brassy in the way men in bars are, boasting. Dad used to call it "bullshitting," and he was an expert. I'm an odd-duck mix of male and female. Like I've been saying, I've always been more my dad's than my mom's. Of course, not until I joined the WACs did I know my options. Dad often said on our trips to deliver welfare to the Indians, or when we ringed pistons in the old Ford, or were ice-fishing, or hunting deer, that I was "the best boy he'd ever had." I glowed. Perhaps in some crazy way, loving him so much, and wanting to be as much like him as possible, jiggled some male hormones and made women excite me.

The New House

OUR SECOND HOUSE was like the first, for it was also of logs with plastered moss. Of course, Bob, you know all this—you were there, too. Add your own touches later if you want.

Remember that small lean-to covered with tarpaper? In there was a kitchen sink with slop bucket and a pitcher pump mounted on a splash board Dad hewed from pine. To the left of the pump hung some slap-dash dish cupboards of apple-box wood thrown together. The door knobs were old sewing thread spools. To decorate the cupboards, Mom clipped Guernsey cows from cans of Whitehouse evaporated milk, a cheap, staple food. Further to the right a metal, V-shaped bin held our flour. Near it was a work area for rolling and kneading bread dough. There was also a cutting board that you pulled out for slicing meat and chopping your vegetables. Below, other shelves held our flour, salt, lard, spices, and the powdered sugar we poured onto the thick fresh cream topping our pancakes.

Our primary source of water was an outdoor cast-iron pump with primer, which in winter we thawed by pouring kettles of boiling water down until the ice cracked loose. Near the pump was a sawed-off half-barrel for watering our cow. Most of the year we hung cuts of meat, cream jars, and home-made butter on ropes inside the well to keep them cool, secure from skunks and rats.

From the outside shed you walked into the kitchen with its old Home Comfort wood-burning range, with warming oven and a reservoir holding lots of warm water. A box for chopped wood, also on the right, resembled a big toy chest without a cover. We all took our turns filling the box with poplar, birch, spruce, and pine. Pine was best for a fast blaze. You, Bob, filled it more than the rest of us did. I loved to perch on the wood box, especially on winter days, close to the stove. One afternoon I was up there reading when I jumped down to go to the outside toilet. Mom was taking a fresh apple pie out of the oven, and I struck the dish, dumping it on the floor. Mom laughed, saying: "Well, tonight we'll have apple upside-down pie."

In our main room stood a round oak table with old-fashioned maple chairs pulled up around it. Remember, Bob, you always had your favorite chair, the one with the funny lyres carved in the back? Mom made you a feather pillow with Dutch boys skating on it. On the table was our single-wick kerosene lamp, shadeless. I hated trimming the wick. To clean soot from inside the glass chimney, I would force wadded newspaper up into the glass, turning it round and round until the lamp was clean. With a pair of scissors, kept for the purpose, I trimmed off all the wick's burned edges so that the flame would be bright. Then I filled the lamp. The smell, sweet and oily, I've never forgotten. And now, whenever I get a whiff of the stuff, it takes me back to childhood. I can still see the pool of light cast by the lamp, an orange turning bright yellow near the base. I don't recall when Dad bought our first Aladdin mantle-lamp, with its wonderful white light, so much easier on the eyes. Those flimsy mantles looked like baby booties. We were getting civilized at last.

To the back of the room, far enough out from the wall so as not to start a fire, was the pot-bellied stove and another wood box crammed with birch and pitch pine. Occasionally, Dad brought bags of cheap coal from Hanke's Coal and Ice, making the banking of fires easier. On those nights when he feared the fire might die, he'd get up, wearing his drop-seat Union underwear, and stoke the fire with slow-burning maple. He'd joke saying that his butt, exposed by the underwear, was freezing. He never minded showing us his crack, though I never once saw his front parts. Did you?

When the fire died, on thirty-below-zero nights, we woke to find frost covering our blankets. Our eyebrows, too, were coated with frost. The water pails and tin dippers were frozen solid. Upstairs, where you and Everett slept under patchwork quilts Mom made from corduroy and wool, the air was coldest. Since Dad never finished insulating the hip-roof, frost-covered nail-heads stuck through the boards an inch or two, and when fire raged in the downstairs heater, the nails dripped into your faces. You guys then jumped from bed in a hurry.

Dad's morning routine made me feel more secure than any one thing in that rough life. He'd rise, switch on the WLS Prairie Farmer Station, Chicago, for Red Foley and Lulu Belle and Scotty, build fires, throw eggs, flour, and milk into the pancake batter he kept souring in a two-gallon crock on the back of the stove, and add more A&P coffee to the pot of sludge he never emptied. Some mornings Mom was so cold (she always wore dresses and aprons—pants suits weren't invented yet) she'd stand by the heater, hike her skirts and warm her backside, then turn, repeating the action, warming her front.

Dad was an early-radio buff, and took a William De Forest home correspondence course. Despite his lousy schooling, two years in a prairie school, he did okay. He was good at math and used colorful images when he talked. With Mom's help, he earned A's on his tests. After a few months though, he quit. There was no money for the tuition.

I remember our first radio, a crystal set with headphones, which meant that only one of us could listen at a time. The static was dreadful. The high point was Kate Smith's famous show, introduced by her theme song: "When the Moon Comes Over the Mountain." Shortly afterwards, Dad bought an early Sears Roebuck Silvertone radio, one run on B-batteries, a radio we all enjoyed. Dad liked the Friday Night Fights. It made him remember, he said, his early years as a boxer at county fairs and carnivals.

We did our damndest to make the house cheerful, despite the

flattened cardboard boxes Dad tacked up to keep snow, rain, and cold from driving through the walls. I've never figured out why he didn't slap up some culled boards, which were cheap at Eagle River Lumber. Maybe since he grew up in sod houses and shacks he didn't know how to make a place livable. Sure, you, Marge, and I could have nailed up weather-boards—but it didn't enter our heads to. That was Dad's work.

One evening Dad came home with wallpaper books, old ones the drugstore was throwing out to make way for the next year's set. These we ripped up, and, matching similar patterns, stirred up a flour paste and covered the walls. Though these didn't keep out much cold, they looked pretty with their flowers, ribbons, and geometric shapes. I liked eating the paste, though Mom said it would glue my guts shut and I wouldn't be able to poop. Dad said we should paste up funny papers, too; we'd have something to laugh at. When the room filled with sunshine, the effect was crazy: each two-by-two-foot square of paper contained a run of matching border which changed the welter of flowers, leaves, and geometric designs into a visual hodgepodge. The flour paste stuck good, until the damp seeped through—which took months. As edges dried, loosened, and turned yellow, we simply smeared on more paste and slapped down new pages.

To get to the bedroom where Marge and I shared that saggy double bed set up near the foot of our folks' bed, you entered a doorless space covered by a flowered curtain—of roses. The tiny room, added on to the main house, was of slender, upright pine logs chinked with moss and plaster. Only behind a white sheet draped between their bed and ours could our parents be private. I'd sleep facing the wall with Marge on the outside, which made it easier for her when she'd been on a date. At times she'd mistake me for her current boyfriend, gangly, shy Hiram Ewald, and clutch me to her, muttering "Hiram, Hiram." Sure, like a good sis, I kept my trap shut. Marge just didn't know what she was doing.

Mom's bed, of wrought iron leaves and roses, stood near a dresser on which she kept bobby pins and combs in a shell once belonging to an unlucky mud turtle wandering up from Mud Minnow Lake to eat our strawberries. Dad found him, chopped off his head, and hung him in a tree until sundown (the usual death hour for turtles). He fleshed the creature, which meant he scraped off all the meat he could, which

Mom cooked. I didn't like it, although Dad believed turtle tasted like turkey, pork, and beef, depending on which part of the animal you ate. By hanging the shell in the sun for a week, you got ants to clean out all the tissue and fat. We lacquered the shell.

Mom displayed her skin and hair care things neatly on a cotton runner she'd embroidered with flowers. Her combs were clean, and I loved the smell of her face-powder, which, as I recall, was Ponds, bought at the local Woolworth's. Her perfume, special, reminded me of what rich women in movies wore with their mink furs and dia-monds.

Above the dresser was her wedding picture, enlarged from a Kodak photo and set in an oval tin frame with stamped, raised flowers and a purple ribbon. Today it hangs over my bed. Mom wears bangs, as the fashion of the twenties was, has a pongee blouse, and stands a few inches below Dad, leaning against him. Dad is handsome with small lips, bright eyes, and hair brushed away from his forehead. He has on a white, dotted string tie. I still have the tie. My older son Marty carried it in his pocket on his wedding day. The picture is hand-tinted, the water-colors still bright. A traveling salesman traded the picture for chickens and eggs rather than money, a common exchange then. Oh, Mom was seventeen and Dad was twenty-one when they got married. You were born a year later. All those years, even after Mom had her hysterectomy when she was thirty-five, Dad never two-timed her. A record, wouldn't you say, living up here?

More Country Matters

OUR NEW HOUSE ran down to a kitchen garden, Mom's straw-berry and rhubarb patch, and a sizeable potato, squash, and corn field. By standing on your toes you glimpsed Mud Minnow Lake half a mile away. Near the vegetable patch was Dad's saw rig, built from an old Model-T engine, pulleys and belts, and a circular saw used to cut trees into lengths for stovewood. In a saw-dust pile we buried ice harvested from the lake, which in summer made delicious blueberry ice-cream and cooled our watermelon and lemonade. Then there was the bloody chopping block, a pine stump, where we beheaded chickens.

Going a bit west you found the outhouse, a two-seater, smelling of lime, urine, and poop, built of slab-wood. In winter you did your business fast, for snow filtered through the walls and covered the seats. Also, the sight through the adjacent seat of a mound of frozen poop piling higher and higher was disgusting. In summer, you stamped your feet to scare off snakes. Each April, Dad excavated the deposits, shoveling all that nitrogen into a wheelbarrow and carting it to the cabbage and vegetable patches. He'd joke that you could always tell the Saturday night deposits; they were the ones full of peanuts. On Saturdays we always shelled peanuts and listened to "The Hit Parade."

All this shocks me now—using human waste to raise food—I'd like to think it didn't happen. But, Bob, we know it did, right? In fact, you helped Dad cart the stuff to the garden. How can poop be good fertilizer, considering the bacteria, microbes, pus, and viruses? Not to mention the undigested scraps of meat gristle and bone. Doesn't "elimination" mean pooping out the poisons? Sure, animals have plenty of germs in their guts—but, at least, those whose wastes we use, the farm beasts, are vegetarians. Maybe that's the difference. I've never gotten used to the smell of human poop, even in baby diapers. Cow manure, though, don't bother me. And when you're wiping yourself and dirty a finger, even after you've washed it, the aroma lingers. It's not fair. I've noticed over the years that not very many farmers have bad feet or sinus problems.

A biker boyfriend once told me about Germany where he served in a WW II tank corps. The local burgomaster, priding himself on having the best garden in the village, had dibs on the rich manure shat by his sausage-loving, beer-sousing citizens. GI tank gunners would train their guns on his "honey buckets" and blast them before he could cart them to the fields.

Remember the fat Sears Roebuck Catalogue we hung on a nail on the outhouse wall? We always thumbed past the colored to the uncolored pages; for the colored ones, slick, did an awful job of wiping. No two-ply paper back then. The only stores even stocking toilet wipe catered to the summer tourist trade. In the catalogue, I'd linger over the bras and panties—they were so delicate and cute, and would wish we could afford them instead of the flour sack ones we wore, bleached and sewn by Mom. Our underskirts were cut from the same stuff.

A few yards on past the privy was the chicken coop and a fenced-in spot where the hens fed and drank. The coop itself was of poplar and birch poles, nailed vertically, forming both roof and sides, with dirt floor, roosts, and egg-laying and nesting boxes. The back of the coop was tight against the log barn where we kept our milk cow and her most recent calf. The latter we raised for a year and then butchered. Twice a year we'd whitewash the coop, which I hated doing since crusty chicken feces stank and was riddled with lice. I usually waited till after setting season; for, not only would I disturb the hens on their nests, but they wouldn't crap for days, and, then, when they climbed out for food and water, they shit mounds of the smelliest poop on planet earth—a hippo with diarrhoea could never stink so much. By drenching the coop with creosote we kept the lice down; for they'd infected a hen's ears, and the ears would bleed, attracting other hens. Within an hour the wretched bird was cannibalized, picked dead. During cold weather, Dad kept a kerosene lantern burning in the coop. Eventually, he buried an old automobile gas tank and stoked it with hardwood coals. It helped, for our hens seldom froze.

One danger, and we lost some birds this way, came from skunks and weasels. They'd dig routes under the coop, enter at night, grab roosting hens and suck out their blood. They'd kill for the hell it, stuffing the gas-tank heater with corpses. Once, Dad yanked out a dozen still-warm hens, which we skinned and canned. Dad never shot any of the varmints with his .22, although he'd wait in the dark for them for hours.

The cow barn, a squat structure of unpeeled logs, stood upright, with a log roof chinked with moss and plaster. You entered through a low door to face a pair of stanchions, one for Lady and the other for her calf. On the wall opposite were two small trap doors which could be raised, enabling us to shovel fresh manure out of the way so that the cow could rest without becoming a shitty mess, spoiling the milk. During the fall and winter months the manure pile grew; there was always enough to fertilize our crops.

We piled hay just outside the barn door for easy forking into the mangers. When all the grasses Dad harvested from our fields and along the roads were eaten, he bought baled hay from local farmers who had surpluses. He extended our supply also by cutting what was called "marsh hay," seeded thick flax-like grasses from the swamps which could shred your hands when you tried to break them off. The cows ate this only when we mixed it with sweeter, more digestible timothy. Today, none of the farm buildings stand, and a single-story, modern house now sits on the foundation of our old house.

Forest Fires

FOREST FIRES were frequent, and scary. One of the largest, in 1948, burned three thousand acres of the Powell Marsh near Manitowish Waters. Four hundred men were on the fire lines. For a week skies over Eagle River were white with ashes. Sunsets were bloody. In 1953, a fire near Spring Lake, in the Nicolet National Forest, ate a thousand acres in two days. If you lived outside the town limits you had no choice but to use your pails and tubs, soaking roofs, or by digging trenches, hoping that the fire would burn crops and outbuildings and die before reaching your house.

In September, 1908, a blaze, probably lightning-caused, began near the Eagle River power dam just south of town. Officials thought it would starve itself; but it didn't. Flames whipped by winds soon reached Eagle River. People watered their roofs. Others took their belongings, put their kids in baby carriages, and crossed the trestle bridge away from town to the north. A Chicago Northwestern train waited near Wall and Main to evacuate folks. According to eyewitnesses, a deluge of rain, a gift from God, doused the fire and saved the town.

A bad recent fire, in May, 1986, once again started in the Nicolet National Forest. This one was stupidly set by forestry workers as a "controlled burn." When the jet stream dropped from twenty thousand to five thousand feet, gusting to eighty-five miles per hour, the storm roared. Soon, over sixty separate fires were out of control. Most of Vilas County seemed doomed. Twenty-man crews were organized, flying into the Rhinelander airport from as far away as Maine. All local able-bodied men volunteered. Within a week the crews held the burn to 1600 acres of trees. Only one two-story home in Conover burned.

Today, each dwelling in Vilas County has a fire control number so that crews can readily locate fires. Much thanks to Paul Trachtenberg for helping me with these details, by fishing them out of the local newspaper "morgue."

Snakes, Frogs, Toads, and Rats

WHILE WE HAVE no poisonous snakes, we've got tons of non-poisonous ones, the garter snake being common. Dad once saved me from a pine snake with a gold ring around its neck. It had slithered into the outhouse. When it started up my leg, I yelled, and Dad rushed over from the barn with a shovel and killed it. We slaughtered all garter snakes, chopping them in half with axes and hoes, not realizing they helped farmers, ridding the area of vermin. We killed no snakes, though, after sundown, on pain of a year's worth of bad luck. Certainly, snakes as creatures of Satan causing the fall of man explained our loathing. Back then you, Bob, were the family Bible-reader. The snake business goes back to Adam and Eve. I won't ask you if you think Eve got a fair shake.

The only garter snake I ever killed I found in our corn patch with a toad stuck in its craw, half in, half out. He was trying to gulp his meal. Feeling sorry for the toad, I figured that if I ground my shoe just behind the snake's jaws the mouth would snap open. It worked, but the toad was already dead.

My brother Everett either twirled snakes by their tails in your face or dropped them down your back. Once when you and I were chopping popple for winter wood, I found a nest of baby garters. On my way back to the pump to fill a peanut butter pail with drinking water, I kicked a rotting log, releasing the massed glob of black spaghetti. With my bare hands I dumped the lot into my empty pail. After waiting till you thought I'd had time to fetch the water, I returned, handing you the bucket. You raised the pail and dumped the snakes all over your face. You didn't think it was funny. I managed to reach the house before you did and crawled under my bed until you'd calmed down.

We hated toads almost as much as snakes. Popular lore said that if a toad peed on you (and the minute you held one it let go no matter how careful you'd been) you got warts. One summer, toads were everywhere, so Marge and I proceeded to see how many we could catch. Since we hated touching them, we captured them with sticks, one on each side, as with chopsticks. After an hour or so we had a dozen. One large toad peed all over my face. The taste was vile, reminding me of those mixtures Everett made me drink. Dad laughed: "Just wash your face good. You won't get warts." I didn't believe him, and for days checked the mirror for ugly bumps.

One afternoon you proudly showed us a pair of mating toads you called "Siamese." You thought you'd discovered a "freak" of biology and would take "it" to your teacher. Dad, laughing, suspended one toad inside a jar, draping the other over the outside. The weight broke them apart. You blushed: toads sure are slow to mate!

There were no better signs of spring than frogs spawning in ponds and ditches. Bull frogs burbled like out-of-tune tubas. Smaller ones were flutes, English horns, or bones scraped over boards. Especially at dusk, their music was wonderful. I could identify singing chats between pairs. Huge jellied placenta-like eggy masses, under water, were attached to dead tree branches, which made dragging them in easy. We hatched tadpoles in fruit jars and bowls. Almost every school year we hatched them. Later, once the tadpoles had grown legs, we dumped them into ponds. Most still kept the shrinking tails they'd used for food.

Frogs were not only play mates but fish bait. We'd thrust the hook under their jaws, and cast them forth to lure bass. One game that you, Everett, and the Jolly boys played was awful. After you'd inserted hollow grasses up the frogs' a-holes, you inflated them with your lips until they either exploded or floated around on the water. To maneuver them you'd tie grass blades to their legs. When Everett tired of floating blown-up frogs he smashed them with rocks.

One afternoon Everett insisted that I help him see how many frogs in roadside ditches we could kill with stones. The first one upset me, for when I pulled him to the bank, he was stretched out on his back with his little hands folded in prayer. I knew that frogs mated for life. I never killed another frog. I believed that inside every frog was a prince.

Rats, though never as bad as a plague, multiplied, especially in the hen-house. They fed on eggs and dead hens. They seldom killed live chickens unless they had croup or fatal lice infections. I feared their yellow teeth and long tails. Shortly before winter, they'd make their way under (and up into) the house where Dad set traps of apple-box wood, supplied with trap doors and mesh-wire cones where he threw wheat and smeared welfare cheese. The rats, usually, were smart enough to trip the door and eat the bait.

One rat worked his way under the house and into our root cellar. How, I never quite understood; for he had to burrow beneath the house. The trap door, cut into the center of the living room (we kept a braided rug over the spot to keep from tripping over it) seemed safe, and was hard to raise up. Dad usually had to do it. One evening as he was about to send me down to fetch carrots for supper (I hated cooked carrots then and still hate them) he shone a flashlight on a rat reared up, baring its teeth.

Dad set yet another trap, brushed mink grease over it to kill our smell, baited it with grain and cheese, and set it on a pile of red potatoes. Each morning, for several days, before he left for work digging ditches on a WPA crew, he checked the trap.

It was mid-morning, as I recall, when you, Mom, and I heard a clatter. "We've caught him," you yelled, yanking up the cellar door. Mom held the flashlight. Inside the trap the crazed rat flung its body, trying to escape. "Pull it up, Bob," Mom said.

You snagged the rope Dad had tied to the trap.

"What next?" I asked.

Mom's idea was that you (although you were lousy with guns—I was better) would fire a .22 slug into its brain, leaving it in the trap.

"Let's dump him in the fire," you said, going to the heater and removing the lid. Mom threw in some pitch pine which sent flames straight up. You jostled the trap, forcing the rat along the screen as it tried to right itself. Its mouth gaped and its beady orange eyes blazed. You placed the trap, door down, over the fire, and, with Mom pushing, freed the door, exposing the rat. When the animal scurried up against the underside of the wooden cover, you beat its feet with a poker, thrusting it screaming into the flames.

2

Barefoot Girl with Cheek of Tan

Y OU PICKED a good cabin, Bob. It's still early for tourists, so you've got a great view of Loon Lake and those big Norways. The space heater's going. I'm glad it was yesterday and not today the flying ant colony thawed and dropped from cracks in the roof, onto the table. I hate bugs. I was going to bring Shadow, knowing you hate dogs. Your creepy dog-hating look makes me shiver. All the mutt wants is to lick your legs. Poor Shadow! She'll be yipping her head off till I get home.

Your coffee's awful, too strong, tastes like leather boots. I usually drag a few coffee beans through some hot water. I'll be peeing like a trout stream's running through me. Problem is, you're so California. Coffee's got to blacken your tastebuds or it's lousy. I've got simple tastes, and I'm too old and cranky to change.

What time is it? Six-thirty. Why am I up so damned early? My eyes are still full of juice. Hear those boats blatting? They're after walleyes. They bite best either at night or early morning. Would you like a mess of fillets for breakfast tomorrow? Son Gus has a bunch in the freezer. Have the grease hot when I get here.

My butt sure likes this couch better than that busted lawn chair by my garage. Those aluminum ridges feel like shark teeth gripping my maiden flesh. I love the quiet—just the clicking of your computer keys. No kids or neighbors. And nobody knows what you and I are up to—special all the way, right? Our secret—and Paul's. You really think there's a publisher who'll publish this stuff? Well, this trip will either jam us closer or fling us apart mortal enemies. So, don't get too snooty. I see pain up the road, blazing eyeballs.

With some expert digging I bet I could come up with stuff in your past that would generate some tears. You're as weepy and sentimental as me, though you make out you're Mr. Cool.

You've rented this cabin for ten days, right? That's enough for lots of blabbing, scribbling, and typing. What I want to do, to keep from being bored telling everything, is to write some scenes, like they came from plays or novels. What do you think? You know more about such stuff, how you actually make a book.

Don't you like those fat robins? They've turned up from half-way around the world. They must wing here from Florida or South America. Who knows? They gorge on angleworms. Look, there's a dozen yanking fat ones out of the sod. You'll never find worms that big in California, I'll bet. Worms don't feel much, I guess. I do shiver when I see one chopped in two with both ends squirming. These mornings the ground's covered. Until noon you have to watch your step.

How long do you think I'll be here? Three hours? I want a cigarette. Yes, I'm nervous. How often do I tell anybody my life-story? Who wants the world snoopin' in their dresser drawers? Three hours is okay. So, if your computer's clicked on, let's go. I'll try not to talk too fast. When we broke off yesterday I was telling about how our farm looked. And there are the school years. Let me tell you how I saw it all, Bob. In some details our stories will agree. But for most of that time you weren't around.

Country School

IN MY school life three things stood out: I had no fear, I had too many accidents, and I hated showing physical affection. Before actually enrolling as a first-grader in the Sundstein School, which all of us kids attended, I visited for a day.

The school itself, you remember, Bob, had one big room for all classes, with the youngest up near the stove, and the oldest, the eighth graders, in the back. There were about twenty kids, depending on who was home with flu or croup. As a one-day visitor, I looked forward to first-grade in the fall.

The teacher, Dolly Spenser, was young and started off, as many did back then, being hired by a school board before earning a teaching degree. They had "Certificates," a way of getting teachers for low pay in back-woods schools. Dolly, I remember, was sure pretty. She welcomed me as a future first-grader. And she was kissy and huggy!

Both you and Marge were ideal students. Mom always bragged about your teaching yourself at three to read from those Shredded Wheat alphabet cards. And before you were four, since you'd read all the Dick-and-Jane books, Dolly enrolled you in first-grade. I can't blame her for thinking I was cut from the same cookie cutter. Also, my carroty hair braids made me look Swiss or German.

I still see blonde Dolly's self-important walk; she'd preen at any moment. And she *would* squeeze me! I must have been shy, so I'd pull back from her embraces. At recess when she played softball with you boys, she felt I was left out, so she stopped pitching, ran over, and grabbed me up in her arms, nuzzling her face against mine. I pulled free and ran to the girls' toilet, where I hid behind the wooden partition that kept out dirty-minded boys. Unable to lure me out, Dolly left me to wait for you to take me home. You liked Pump Pump Pull-Away, I remember, where you threw a ball over the school roof to "the other side," who caught it, dashed around the building, and hid the ball.

For that school year, whenever Dolly drove by our farm on the way to teach, she honked her horn and waved. One evening she drove up in a new dark blue Model-A coupe with two silver radiator caps. She motioned me over from where I was digging around the bachelor buttons in Mom's flower garden.

"Nellie," she said, climbing out of the car, "I won't be your teacher next year. I'm getting married. I hope you'll like school." She grabbed my hand.

The next year produced Mr. Frank Brown. The year proved our last, for the Sundstein District had such a low enrollment the school board closed it. We were bused five miles away to a new school, the Bohemian. In the meantime, we had to make do with Mr. Brown.

Brotherly Love

"EVERETT PETERS! Get up here!" Teacher Frank Brown was scared of Everett, who had just cursed him, calling him a "cocksucker," a name I'd never heard before.

Everett, a fifth-grader, was taller than Brown, who was short, stocky, with chestnut-colored waves so neat you knew he spent his weekends in hair curlers. He dressed spiffy, in dark blue suit and red tie, and wore shiny oxfords which he spared from mud and slush with slick, black rubbers.

He'd taken a lot of crap from Everett, and, in fact, seemed afraid of fighting the string-bean boy with the dirty mouth. He even sucked up to him by saying that if he did his studies all week he could go home early on Fridays. Everett just stared at the man through his heavy glasses and set his chin harder. He despised the Friday carrot and left school on any day at any time he chose. If Brown followed him to the door, using more dirty words and flailing his arms like a windmill, Everett chased him back inside. Brown shrugged his shoulders and gave in.

This teacher had crushes on both Celia Kula and Helen Jolly, and on me. Although I was only a first-grader, each morning he'd grab me up, pigtails and all, for a vigorous whisker rub. He may have looked clean-shaven, yet his face was sandpaper. After a few days of this, I groused to Dad, who said I should "kick him in the nuts." One blow caused him to yowl like a stuck pig. Everett, standing by, rushed over. If he hadn't, Brown would have thrashed me.

One day, just before lunch, Brown was at his desk waiting for Everett to make a move. I knew there'd be no backing off. Brown rose and grabbed Everett, pulling his arms back behind him, the way wrestlers do before they pin their enemy. With Everett immobilized, Brown slammed him against the blackboard. Everett was stunned. He threw up his hands in defense. He seemed hurt. His glasses flew off. I leapt onto Brown's back, which gave Everett time to wade in with a strong body punch. Brown collapsed on the floor. Henry and Herbie Jolly locked their arms in Everett's and pulled him off. I was really scared, for never in my life had I attacked an adult. Brown got up, walked over to the door and said: "Both of you, leave, now! I'll be seeing your dad, and the Superintendent. You'll be thrown out of this school."

Two days later, Brown arranged a meeting with me, Austin (the Superintendent of Schools), my dad, and himself. When I asked Dad what a "cocksucker" was, he said it was "dirty"; no girl should use it. He didn't know where Everett got it, probably from the Jollys. Filthy words weren't like soap in our brother's mouth, for he hardly ever said a sentence without them.

Everett was expelled to attend a government-run camp for delinquents, Camp Ojibwa, in Oneida County. He spent his days planting trees and in physical exercise—jogging and push-ups. You recall, Bob, that we didn't miss him much. I felt free; but then you always got along with him, although I remember some of those mornings when his teeth shone as he told the folks you'd been "dirty" in bed. Sure, you always denied it.

We both know that Everett hated Dad, boasting that when he was big enough, he'd "beat the shit out of him." Mom usually took Everett's side, feeling guilty for having tried to abort him. Everett's mild epilepsy also bothered her. He'd suddenly fall down, his eyelids fluttering. He grew out of the seizures. When he was six his foreskin shut. The doctor had to cut his skin so he could pee. I was told it was sebum, or smegma, that collected and got infected. I was worried when Dad returned from Doc Barney's with Everett in his arms. When I saw the bandages I knew something was wrong.

Everett always needed to bug somebody. His sense of right and wrong was rotten—he seemed a-moral, rather than non-moral. Norman Botteron, who was your age, would say: "Look at Everett. He can jump off the roof." Right away Everett dashed up and jumped.

He always abused me, more so as we got older. He'd never sit next to me at supper, and he'd start real fights, pounding my back or head, telling Mom I was to blame. And she believed him! At times, Mom had to use a broom to stop his torments.

When I got the used bike I mentioned earlier, he decided it was more his than mine; I could ride it only if I'd do his chores. He always made the rules. One was that I should ride my bike by starting it off on a run and then jumping up, something I never learned to do. Sure, I'd clean the barn for him, water and feed the cow, fork in straw for bedding, and fetch the nightly wood supply for both living room and kitchen stoves. After all that work I'd earned a long bike ride. But I was never sure; more often than not he wouldn't cooperate.

On days we walked to town for a movie, Mom always gave Everett the money. He made me wait for ten minutes before I set out; he didn't want to be seen with me. Once in town, he'd walk on the far side of the street. His sickest trick—and remember, he had the admission money and I wanted to see the show and have my Cracker Jack— was to force me into the undertaker's parlor where I had to kiss a corpse. He'd first go into the rooms to find the oldest and ugliest "remains." Then, looking mean, he'd motion me in, insisting that I plant my lips firmly on both forehead and mouth. I had to do it, or there'd be no movie; so I'd shut my eyes and afterwards run out into the street. To this day I can feel those icy lips, and the mix of smells, the worst being the stink of rotten meat, which neither the formaldehyde nor violet-scented water could conceal.

On our last visit, Griffin, the owner, wanted to know what we were doing; and when he saw Everett standing there with his hat on his head lacking respect for the dead, he ordered us out. I was sure he'd watched us from behind the purple curtains; the light shed from behind the caskets showed him just when my lips touched the corpse. On this last trip, as we were going out the door, I saw him rearranging the casket frills which I'd messed up.

Once inside the Vilas Theater, Everett bought the tickets, gave me mine, then entered alone, forcing me to sit as far away as possible. After the movie, the same procedure: I started for home only after he was well on up the road.

A few more things: he'd mix brews and threaten to beat me if I didn't drink them. The worst was a mix of gas and tractor oil, which I had to down by spoonfuls. He'd also force me to drink a bitter concoction of tomato, white birch, and mullein leaves. Mom, defending him, said he hadn't actually dumped the stuff down my throat—I had. Often he'd find where our new electric cow-pasture fence had the strongest jolts and make me grab the wires. I found out that by putting one hand over the other, the jolts lessened.

Dad was of little help, for he was always at work. And you, Bob, were off at school or with the Insurance company in Wausau, or you'd already gone to the Army. There were times, especially after Everett dropped out of school for good, when he provoked Dad by shoving and calling him foul names.

One morning, when Everett, upstairs, started yelling obscenities, Dad started to grab him. They tangled half-way down the stairs. Mom was bawling her eyes out, pleading with Dad not to hurt Everett. This time Everett lost. He left home and rarely came back.

The Bohemian School

THE BOHEMIAN SCHOOL, also a one-roomer, five miles from home, was in an area of families from Central Europe rather than Germany and Scandinavia. The seating arrangements were like Sundstein's, and a free-standing furnace covered by ornamental tin sheeting stood up where the smallest children sat. The teacher's desk was angled so she could keep her eyes peeled. Near her a set of wooden shelves contained a few text books, a rickety Compton's Encyclopedia, and some classics. The Unabridged Webster's Dictionary stood on a stand and was scribbled where boys had underlined the smutty words. Enrollment was bigger than at Sundstein (thirty children rather than twenty), and for the first time I met Indians from the area, living in conditions much worse than ours.

The bus, driven by Tony Dolansky, served both grade- and high-school students. We were first to be picked up, and after Dolansky dumped us at Bohemian he continued, picking up high schoolers and driving on to town. Once there, he fetched more lower grade students and the teacher Mrs. Victoria Peale. Those of us dropped off shortly after 7:30 a.m. had to wait without an adult in charge for over an hour. Fortunately, Mr. Polachek, a farmer near the school, was the janitor, so the school room was always toasty. Also, anybody getting sick could run to his farm and he would drive them home.

In the evening, Dolansky loaded high-schoolers first, dropping the Bohemian kids off on his way into town. Mrs. Peale rode along, which meant that again us Sundstein kids stayed behind alone. We were lucky to be home by 5:30. In winter it was already pitch-dark by 5.

The hours we waited for Dolansky's bus were hard, especially during cold weather. Locked indoors, the kids shouted, wrestled, and teased one another, tormenting any shy or frightened kids. Bedlam. Some of the older boys and girls were already into necking, which they carried on in the coat room, with one of their group on guard outside the door.

Mrs. Peale was well over six feet tall, horse-faced, and with huge feet shoved into shiny leather nurse's shoes, with bunions. Her salt-and-pepper hair was drawn back in a bun, like Margaret Hamilton's in "The Wizard of Oz." Her lips were crooked, with carmine lipstick. Her beady eyes stared from behind thick glasses. We older kids had to teach ourselves while she focused on the lower grades. We gave ourselves high marks whether we deserved them or not. Mrs. Peale never caught on. She was pretty lazy.

Occasionally a county nurse visited to check for head lice, scurvy, and measles. She bought gallon-sized cans of government surplus baked beans for us to eat. She was right; some of us weren't getting enough food at home. Once when Mrs. Peale forgot to plug air holes in the tins before heating them, they exploded. After a goiter scare we swallowed iodine pills every Friday. As for lice, I was sent home when the nurse saw things crawling on the back of my neck. I'm sure the lice came from sitting near Masseline Deverney, a chunky Indian fifth-grader. I'd seen white specks about a sixteenth of an inch long, dandruff bits, jumping around in her black hair. Mrs. Peale sent Masseline home, and had the County Nurse check the rest of us. Unfortunately, as a host myself, I was embarrassed, feeling filthy. Mom washed my hair in kerosene and used plenty of hot towels, which killed the creatures. Later, we put paper on the living room floor, and Mom, using a fine-toothed comb, loosened dozens of dead lice. There were follow-up treatments for eggs left behind on my scalp. I never want to go through that again.

Mrs. Peale arranged for play equipment like that the town schools had. Since her husband was a high-school biology teacher, she knew you could get stuff if you lived in a school district with rich kids. We now had baseballs and bats. When she brought a football, the bullies ruined it by throwing it against spikes in a post. My Uncle Pete built a teeter-totter, which we loved. Soon we had swings.

While primers were free, we had to buy our own Crayolas, pencils, pens, and paper. Mrs. Peale's punishment for whispering was to force us to write "I Will Not Whisper" five hundred times. She also forced us to copy whole pages from the dictionary. Our signal for going to the toilet was to hold up a single finger for urinating, and two for pooping. I hated this, for you were telling your business to the whole school. The outhouses lacked any kind of paper, rough or smooth, for butt wipe. Unless it was winter, we'd take in a handful of leaves or grass to use.

Willard LaCrosse, a scrawny second-grader from a broken home, gentle and sweet, was hated by Mrs. Peale and the older boys. Once the bullies took bologna from his sandwich, put in earthworms, and forced him to eat it. He gained some respect one morning when Mrs. Peale refused to let him go to the toilet. He strode up to her desk, whipped out his penis, and peed in her waste basket. Afterwards she cuffed him and flung him into his seat.

While Mrs. Peale never berated any of us for being poor, the mere presence of the Seifert and Swett kids stressed our poverty. While Mom saw to it that we were scrubbed and our clothes clean, we never escaped the poverty stigma. It's like we hung signs around our necks, the way blind people do, announcing our bad luck and begging for sympathy. The Seifert family owned a big dairy near the river, and Ray Swett had a permanent job maintaining roads for Vilas County. On the birthdays of these kids, the parents sent ice cream, cake, and cookies. This is when I ate ice cream served in Dixie cups for the first time.

My love for sports, once I had escaped the lower grades, passing with moderate results, grew. I was good at baseball, so good, in fact, that the boys chose me for their teams as much as they chose males. I could hit home runs, yell, field balls, and pitch. When we played hard-ball without gloves, my fingers smarted like they'd been smacked with whips. Usually I wore overalls, t-shirts, and black and white saddle shoes. Few girls dressed this way, preferring the usual frocks and curled hair expected of their sex. Yes, I didn't care much for dolls, especially the dumb ones with blonde hair that said "Ma Ma" and wet their pants.

Treated as a boy by the boys, I was never a sexy flirt and I never played sugary sweet. I never talked real dirty, though—just enough to give some spice to life. If they put me down as a girl I'd sass them. I developed more strength than most girls ever do. The boys loved it when I championed some younger, weaker classmate (male or female) who was being teased or beaten. I'd clean the tormentor's clock.

One bully was Henry Jolly. Coming from a family of eleven kids, he was the family Hercules; if you threatened a Jolly, he'd attack you. Though I never understood why, I was often his victim until, after Dad taught me some boxing punches and wrestling holds, I faced him. As soon as we stepped out of the bus that morning, I called out: "Henry," I said. "Here's a present for you." I launched a hooker, jabbing him so hard in the face his nose bled. Later that morning when another bully, Bobby Swett, arrived, I lit into him. Mrs. Peale never punished me for fighting, and even asked me to guard the younger kids during those morning and late afternoon hours. I guess I should have been paid. Wasn't I doing her work?

Dad's Girl

AS I THINK back over these years, Bob, I'm trying to understand why my psyche was so male. My breasts were developing into the size most girls envy. But I didn't seem to excite any guys. Maybe it was the freckles smeared all over my face and arms. Did I feel much for guys? Not really. You know darn well that Mom and Dad never talked sex with us. And I never once heard them having "it" in bed, did you? I never saw either of our folks naked, even once, except for Dad's butt crack, a standard winter morning feature as he wandered about lighting fires. The only naked male I saw before I married Kovisto was a cherry-picker dude jerking off in a barn. And not until I got to high school and was forced to take gym did I see naked girls. My feelings for women were as stifled as my feelings for guys. I picked up attitudes from Mom: men to her were "dirty," and her favorite nickname for Dad was "Dirty Old Pup." Sure, she'd say this with love, but our brains, yours and mine, must have been influenced. I'd as soon go to bed with a pine board as sleep with a man. Despite all my babies, and men, I never once had an orgasm. For years I didn't know a woman could have one. I sure was in the dark ages. I could never be a "bull dyke." My heart's too much on my sleeve, a quality all women are supposed to have.

My obsession with Dad still puzzles me. I sure never felt sexual. Do you think that my being a tomboy satisfied his wanting a "real" son. You and Everett never fit the bill, and you were much closer to Mom than Dad. Dad, in fact, used to pair you almost as if you were the man and he was your son. Dad never resented your lying in a hammock reading Mom's *True Story Magazine* or *Readers Digest* rather than helping fix cars, hunting, or chopping wood. And he encouraged your education, taught you how to play a guitar, and praised you for not having to spend your life digging ditches as he had to. He was always proud of you.

I shared more of Dad's life, though, than you did. He taught me to use tools, to hunt and fish, to strip junked cars, and to slug beer. He'd take me with him to the Northwoods tavern, his favorite bar, where he "bullshitted" with other men. I learned male boasting, a side of him you always hated. While Dad urged you to fight other boys, he never gave you real tips, as he did me, on blows and wrestling holds. You told me of your nightmares back then where some bully was set to attack and you froze and couldn't get your hands up to defend yourself. Dad often boasted how he was going to knock so-and-so's "block off," how he wasn't going to take "no more shit" from some boss he felt "hated his guts." Yet, he seldom carried out his threats; he merely pumped up his ego to impress Mom and us kids. Nobody was better at bullshitting than Pa. You return another guy's bluff, topping him so he has no comeback. Then he treats you to a beer. Women past a certain age, say twenty-five, behave likewise, though the young ones are supposed to be like kewpie dolls, coy and dumb. I caught on to bullshitting early, and had a great teacher in Dad. The men I've always gotten on best with were bullshitters.

I was always intimidated by Mom, and never felt at ease with her, as I did with Dad. She was beautiful, and though she seldom tossed much physical affection our way, she loved us—I knew that; but she liked you more than the rest of us. Now, don't deny it, she did.

Remember how neat she always was. Each Friday she had a bath, wore a freshly ironed dress, and curled her hair with those wave-makers popular in the twenties. The look was like Clara Bow's hair crimped in waves rather than curled. She liked bangs. On Fridays she always cooked a good meal, with a fresh crumb-top apple pie. Since my folks had no social life, Mom's primping showed Dad she cared. Yet, she was a woman of moods, and when she was lonely she'd perch on a huge grey boulder behind the house until she felt better. In years to come Everett bought the forty and when he left Wisconsin, I lived there with my kids after divorcing Bill. Gus broke his arm, falling off Mom's rock. I still go there, with the remains of the old houses we lived in tumbled into the brush, and think about our lives. Though Marge inherited Mom's looks, I don't think I was ever jealous, and was, in fact, proud of both her and Mom. I liked our family jaunts to town.

I'm not perfect, Bob. I'm sentimental. I can really turn on the tears, worse than a faucet. I also smother my kids and grandkids. Why do I feel so responsible? It's stupid. I can't spare them their miseries. My head hurts thinking about it. Yes, and I smoke too much, although I've cut out beer, and I once drank as if there'd be no tomorrow.

A final note: most of Dad's tools are lying around my garage. When I'm depressed I go out and look at them. It's as though Dad's there beside me saying: "It's alright, Nellie."

Birds and Bees and the Evergreen Trees

MY KNOWLEDGE of babies was weak. When Mom had Jane at St. Mary's Hospital I was eight. Dad told me Mom was going over to pick out a name for a new baby from a list the Catholic nuns kept. I imagined that a mom-to-be walked in and faced cribs of infants waiting to be claimed. You made your choice, stayed a few days to get the baby's formula right, selected a nun-supplied name, then went home. Apparently, Mom's bloated belly made no impression on me. True, Dad told me not to hug her too hard around the middle. Nor did I understand why she stayed in Rhinelander for five days after she'd picked out my sister. "Will Mom still like me when she comes home?" I asked.

"Yes," Dad said. "Why?"

"Well," I explained, "Everett said she'd sell me to gypsies, and if that didn't work, Everett would take me for a ride, dump the boat, and pretend it was an accident."

Although I huddled up to Mom and the new baby in the car, I don't recall even looking over at Jane. At home, I sat by the kitchen table feeling lost. Dad, who usually kissed me good night, didn't notice when I left the room.

Two summers before Jane's birth, Mom had a goiter cut out. For over a year, an egg-sized swelling grew to grapefruit size, squishy with gelatin. I knew the goiter would be removed, and I was scared, for I thought the doctor would lop off Mom's head, dig out the goiter, and then sew her head back on. What if they sewed it on backwards? I've always had a busy mind.

I was as dumb about the facts of sex as about birth. We never talked about it at home, and none of the girls at school said much. Somewhere along the line I learned that boys play with themselves until batches of stuff hit their bellies. Yuck! I never realized that girls, by poking their fingers in and wiggling around, could have fun too. I didn't much like even looking down there. I once saw Everett's thing—he was seven or eight when his skin grew shut and he was circumcised (I used to say *circumscribe*). I watched Mom change his bandages. He yelled when he saw me. I didn't see much except for a funny bit of swelled-up skin.

And I saw roosters mount hens. When our rooster Crip rode a biddy, I thought he'd kill her. Why did she give in so easy? She just squatted in the dirt and let him grab her comb and tread her. Once Crip got off, I saw the hen's anus twitching. I realized that with chickens it all depends on the timing—if fertilizing happens. I've never figured out what exactly a rooster shoves up a hen, have you? For when I butcher them I find the gonad beans but never any penises. Even cut-up birds bought at a store often have them attached to the rib cavity below the lung tissue. Though I'm told that a cock actually glues the rim of his anus to the hen's, I just don't believe it. What if us humans had to do that? Those positions would be weird! When I threw stones at Crip he'd jump off and run through the pigweed ruffling his feathers, staring at me with that awful red eye. Though his toes froze off one arctic night, he liked chasing me. When Lady, our cow, was "in heat," Dad led her across the road to Kaminsky's bull. When they returned there was lots of mucus dripping from her vagina. Perhaps if boys had found me sexy, as they did Marge, I might have been wiser and not the butt of so many of their smutty jokes.

For the most part, I ignored changes in my body. One day Mom jolted me: "With our next order to Sears we'll get you a bra. You're ready." She also explained that I'd soon get the "curse." "All girls go through this," Mom said. She was glad, she told me, they'd invented Kotex; when she was a girl they used flannel rags which she'd wash and use and reuse. I never knew that any liquids except pee ran out of us females, and, yes, Mom told me that after pooping I should wipe away from my vagina, away from the bacteria. I've always been careful about my hygiene and dread Kotex breath.

Let me try something on you, Bob. If you're a girl and you have a mom and a sis who are prettier than you, you can't feel as close to them, say, as you do to your dad and brothers. You grew up to crave the approval of women more than men. Hear what I'm saying? To me, being noticed by a woman is a hundred times better than by a man. Transfer this idea to you: Dad was so physical, and you by failing to reflect his image, longed for other men to find you masculine. Oh, shit! I don't know what I'm talking about. So let's go on to something else, like my first period?

One July afternoon, in the kitchen, I was waiting to go with Mom to pick strawberries. She was wiping the lunch dishes and had just prepared a beef stew. Suddenly, something warm and sticky ran down my legs. "Mom, Mom," I shouted, pointing towards the blood.

She touched my shoulder. "It's come," she said. "That's your period. We'll fix it."

She wadded a dishtowel between my legs and led me to her bedroom where, after washing me with soap and water, she gave me a sanitary napkin and belt and put me to bed. Blood flowed for almost two days. Mom promised it would end and that I'd be OK for another month. During most of my periods, I've had much blood and severe cramps. Only Mydols helped.

After my menstrual clock was set, I feared going to school. Not only was I too shy to buy Kotex (Mom was too, so Dad usually bought it, calling it "cornflakes"), but I never used the coin machines, dreading my class mates' knowing. As it was, I was teased enough for my freckles.

Mom should have explained to me how males make babies. But she didn't. My sex education was foul, and so was yours, Bob. You say that Dad delivered his only sex spiel to you (two sentences) when Marge first menstruated. Since Mom was then in the hospital having her goiter removed, Dad sent her up to Aunt Kate for advice. That same day he told you to go across the road and take Celia Kaminsky into the brush. "Do what a bull does to a cow. Flop Celia on her back." I guess he didn't know better. If your sex education was bad, imagine what his was like.

So, why blame the folks? That's how they were raised. And sure, if I'd had a bosom pal or two, females, before I was a sophomore in high school, I might have picked up a few clues. You had the Jollys, right, and the four of you played in their hayloft, and then the Army came along. You and me were late bloomers. Well, there's no use sittin' here with all that sunshine peeking through the picture window. You can wallow in self-pity; I'm not going to. Are you ready for more of the story? Let me grab some fresh coffee first.

During high school I read a lot, mostly novels from the public library housed in a tiny City Hall room. My plan was to start with A and go to Z, a plan not made to please teachers, but to please yours truly. I'd read all the books you and Marge read. The public library was more anonymous than high school, which didn't have many books anyhow, other than those dumb textbooks. I loved *For Whom the Bell Tolls*, *Fair Stood the Wind For France*, and *God's Little Acre*. How neat when Hemingway's hero blows up the enemy bridge! I also fantasized about the heroine Maria. Ingrid Bergman played Maria, and Gary Cooper the hero. The story's still fantastic. *God's Little Acre* struck me, where the stranger drives up to the sharecropper hovel where Darling Jill lies wriggling in the dust while the stranger barters for her. After Jill's "deflowered" she lays there in the sun while a trail of ants criss-crosses her belly. These books didn't give me much hard information, but they did feed my dreams. And that's why all my life I've read. A fantasy is about as good as the real thing. Seeing it like this you don't end up feeling sorry for having got the short end of the stick. My favorite author is Katherine Forrest, the lesbian novelist. You've gotten some of her books, and I've ordered more. They're all back in my bedroom. Forrest's detective Kate Delafield really stirs me. I've even cooked up stories myself; perhaps I'll jot them down and send them to her. Might even get a reply. You know her, don't you?

I was so bored in high school. I preferred typing to home economics, manual arts to history. You remember Mrs. Hanke, that history teacher who hired you to correct her papers? You were her pet. She sure hated me, and all because she decided I was dumb. "Hands-on learning" is my thing. Give me a kitchen sink to stick together; I'll throw away the instruction book and figure out by myself just how the parts work, how the hardware clunks in to get the water running right.

Yet, my idea of love, romanticized, mostly came from books, and, yes, from talking to Shelley Congleton, Victoria Dolansky, and Dolores Birch. These gals were always giggling over their latest male. Love was supposed to blast us females off to bliss. But how? Males set women's juices flowing in an *orgasm*—a word not in my vocabulary back then.

When Hurley Remington touched my hand at the County Fair (I was a junior in high school), doors swung open. There was also that walk in a woods with you, Bob. On one of your visits home from college we talked about our lives. That evening, the early May air was clear and crisp. We reached Silver Lake, just past the high school, the swimming spot popular with teenagers.

"Nell, I'm worried that you don't care enough about boys. You're almost seventeen." When you said I had an attractive body, I didn't know what to say.

"Well," I remember replying: "I do wish some lotion would bleach these freckles." I used to cringe, thinking that in morning assembly the principal would announce a contest for the student with the most spots. He'd call up Melvin Brown, a math brain, to make a count, limiting his attention to one forearm per student and one side of a face.

You laughed. "That's a start. There's more?"

I know you're sick of my saying I never wanted breasts. I could barely stand to see them in a mirror and even tied them down with cloth. They were the tops of inflated plastic ice cream cones, like those you tack up to advertise a fast-food stand. Or, they were overblown muffins. Full-sized men's shirts hid them pretty well. I avoided showers after gym as much as I could; fortunately, we could play baseball in regular clothes instead of stripping in a locker room, as we did for volleyball and basketball. If you lived in town, showers were not required. No stranger ever saw me naked until I joined the WACs.

"Go after some boys," you persisted. "Mom married when she was barely seventeen. And I was already in the oven. . . ."

"Mom had sisters close to her age. . . ."

"Yet, they, too, lived on a farm, ignorant.

You were right, for when Mom turned sixteen, her mother said there were too many mouths to feed—there were seven sisters and four brothers, and she either had to go to Fargo and work or get married. She'd finished one year in high school. So when Dad came along she married him. We thought the hysterectomy finished her as a sexual person. She hated all the pregnancies and miscarriages. She'd say she was a *man*—that's the word she used, and that's why she and Dad slept in different rooms. My guess is that she never had any real sex fun. Her generation saw sex for creating kids.

Just look what happened to my girlfriends: Sylvia Dolansky ended up pregnant, Jane Jones married before she was twenty, and Dolores Birch moved to another state to have a baby. Only Shelley Congleton broke the mold by joining the Army and became a Captain. She was another red-head, taller than me by six inches, with small lips and a pout I liked, and eyes that looked like they'd start laughing. She was sexy in a skirt and blouse. A plaid skirt with gores high-lighted her plump butt. If I could then have put my feelings for her into words, I'd have honored my crush, one deeper than I'd ever had on a boy. Sure, I'd been jealous of the boys and girls who paired off and had swimming dates. But I've never been too bored with my own company.

"I'm not a freak, Bob." I picked up a pebble and skimmed it over the lake, making a perfect arc. "I'll just have to wait and see what happens. So far, no boy has asked me out." You knew I wasn't telling the whole truth, right?

"That's self-protection," you said. "It's that simple."

I'd never be pretty, as Marge was. Georgia Hanke once stopped me in the school corridor: "Nell, what happened? Your older brother got all the brains, and your sister got the looks."

"My dad says that my beauty shines from the inside out, not from the outside in," I snapped at her.

We, you and I, sat there side by side at that picnic table by the lake, both of us quiet.

"I almost wish I wasn't a woman," I said. You, always the listener, waited for me to go on. "I hate dresses," I said. On a few occasions—graduation was one—when I had to wear a dress, I ached to rush home and throw on overalls. I also despised having my hair curled and smearing on lipstick. Somewhere inside me peculiar genes were bubbling to the surface, threatening to take over.

3

The Joys of Primitive Cooking

Bringing in the Sheaves

YOU'LL LOVE these walleye fillets, Bob. I pulled them out of the freezer last night. I'm frying them in egg and mushroom soup batter, with crushed cornflakes, a touch of pepper and cinnamon, and sizzling grease. The trick is to get 'em golden brown. Sit down at the table. The first batch is ready.

I can tell you're a Peters—you love your food! And your belly's almost as big as mine. Wet cement. No matter how poor we were, there was always food, plenty of it to go around. This hot grease takes me back to those eggs we fried every morning, fresh from the nests. I loved 'em, and when nobody was looking, I'd down six fried so crisp their edges were like hard brown lace. Plenty of salt, plenty of pepper. After the eggs cooked, we'd toss slices of home-made bread in, frying them, smearing them with home-churned butter and dollops of Mom's pincherry jelly or strawberry jam . . . and then the crisp bacon from our own pig . . . and Dad's daily sour-dough pancakes.

You never liked the pancakes. I always felt I'd hurt Dad's feelings if I didn't eat 'em. I guess my guts were more cast iron than yours. I got used to 'em.

Aren't these walleyes tasty? Here's more. Eat up.

Remember all the welfare peanut butter we ate doubling it with hot bacon drippings? We'd set a lard pail half full of peanut butter on the stove to get soft, then stir in the grease. Salty, smoky, and great for sandwiches. When that ran out, we ate sandwiches smeared with plain lard and slabs of onion-fried potatoes.

Lady's cream we churned in a gallon-sized square jar with screw-on top and wooden paddles. None of us was too anxious to whirl the handle, but whoever did got to drink the buttermilk.

Whenever Lady's cream dried up, Dad bought oleo, which in those days could not be sold colored since it would resemble butter, something the Wisconsin Dairy lobby nixed. After all, Wisconsin was "The Dairy State." We spooned the pale oleo into a bowl, crushed in a bead of orange dye, and colored it like butter. At school, our oleo sandwiches told the other kids who had plain lard sandwiches we were eating better than they were. A hinged, four-sided, wooden mold formed neat one-pound slabs. With a knife you scraped the excess, opened the mold, dumped the brick onto waxed paper, and set it in a cool place. Lard was our cooking staple.

A milk by-product was cottage cheese, which Mom made in a pan on the stove. Once the milk soured and curdled, she dumped it into cheese-cloth and hung it dripping over a bowl. We ate the cheese sprinkled with brown sugar, cinnamon, and welfare raisins. We ate a lot of this, too much for me. You'd have to hold me down to stuff cottage cheese in my mouth.

No bread today tastes as good as that Mom baked in the old Home Comfort stove. Twice a week she'd mix flour from the fifty-pound government surplus cloth bags with yeast dissolved in boiled potato water. She set the dough in one of the warming closets of the kitchen range. Later, when she punched and shaped the dough into loaves and rolls, she stoked the wood fire and stuck them in the oven. You were in charge of the wood. Small chunks of pitchpine gave the best heat. She always set a pan of water with the bread, which hardened the crust. The heels fresh from the oven were delicious. I'm salivating.

I never got my fill of her cream puffs. They were special, remember, stuffed with cream whipped with a hand beater. Then, her great raisin-filled cookies? Starting with a basic white dough she'd cut two-inch circles. In a hand grinder she'd mix raisins with sugar, smearing rounds of dough with the cooked raisin mixture, then topping it, sealing it with a fork. She also baked rolls smeared with egg yolk and poppy seeds, seeds picked from our own flowers. It's illegal any more to grow them. Mom also loved morning glories, another plant you can't grow. In the 'sixties hippies discovered you got high from them. A cheap food was popcorn. After a few attempts to grow some, we gave up, for, while ears formed, none of the kernels popped. We never solved that one. Perhaps our soil was wrong. We wasted nothing: even the "old maids" left after popping we put through a grinder and mixed with Karo syrup.

Twice a month we had cherry cakes of lard or bacon drippings, cocoa, and icings of powdered sugar colored and mixed with cream. Marge and I ate tablespoons of sugar while mixing the batter. I liked Betty Crocker's recipes. They came in bags of Pilsbury flour. One cake was a checkerboard (thanks again to B.C.) where you swirled cocoa or red dye through white dough.

The worst cakes I ever tasted were Aunt Kate's. They were somewhere between bread and cookie dough. She filled rectangular pans with the odd dough, baked it, and topped it with half an inch of powdered sugar colored purple, green, and bright orange. Dad said her being French Canadian explained the bright colors. You see them on blankets and squaw clothes. Her frostings were like clay.

When we started on this story, Bob, you joked we should call it "A Wisconsin Pancake Saga," for Dad ate pancakes every morning of his life, starting when he was a tot on the prairie. His dad would leave him for days in their sod house with nothing to eat but pancakes cooked on a wood heater. You used to fuss at him for never washing the crock he kept the batter souring in. He was sure mad when you did clean it: that rancid batter was gold, and you'd destroyed the yeast. Each morning he added more flour, eggs, drippings, and baking powder. The cakes had the texture of cardboard. Until he died he never missed a day of pancakes smeared with sugar and cream, or jam and peanut butter, with bacon, pork chops, or venison on the side.

I also remember our taffy pulls. We boiled the sugar and butter to the hard-ball stage. After the mixture cooled, with greased hands we pulled the stuff into supple braids, which we marked with a knife for easy breaking, and set in the snow on the roof.

We'd no notion of vegetarianism, and to think of meatless days, even when the war was on, stirred our self-pity—we might starve if we didn't have red meat. Even chicken was no substitute for beef, venison, or pork—it didn't stick to your ribs, Dad would say. So, we saw few meatless days. We did eat a lot of fish, much of it caught through the ice. Also, we received U.S. Department of Agriculture doles of Argentinean canned beef, delivered in olive drab tins stamped "Not to be Sold: USDA." We cooked the meat with canned peas or corn, and even ate it, thick fat and all, directly from the can. We both loved chicken, and though we used hens primarily for eggs, we raised friers and made stew when the hens stopped laying. In late summer we culled the cockerels, keeping one rooster alive to help Old Crip service the hens. Each fall Mom canned over a hundred quarts of chicken.

We were not much for fresh vegetables, though in summer and fall we enjoyed corn on the cob, radishes, green onions, and lettuce. We enjoyed Mom's pickled beets and cucumbers, and the sauerkraut Dad fermented in a twenty-gallon crock. We ate lettuce either wilted with bacon grease or drowned in milk and cream sweetened with Karo syrup. Even if we had craved fresh vegetables out of season there were none in the stores; and bananas, oranges, and apples were so expensive we ate them only at Christmas.

As I chat about food, I see how important Minnow Lake was, and how lucky we were that it was so near, only fifteen minutes away. You are right; we didn't develop it as we could have. The bloodsuckers were too thick for swimming, and until Dad and Uncle Pete planted bass fingerlings nothing grew there but mud turtles and those stupid tiny yellow perch. And we never had a decent boat. The fingerlings ate up the bloodsuckers. I sure hated those critturs, how they'd glue themselves to your skin and suck your blood. The only way we got them loose was with lighted matches.

Eventually we caught tons of fish in Minnow Lake—crappies, bass, and bluegills, all free for the time it took to throw out baited lines and yank them in. I love just saying the names of local plants and shrubs: hazelnut, blackberry, sumac, wintergreen, and the trailing arbutus we picked and sold, the princess pine feathery and great for wreaths, creeping jenny, skunk cabbage with the stinky juice we rubbed on each other's cheeks, starflower moss, white water lilies, cranberry shrub blossoms drooping over into the ice-cold lake. All this nature seen up close against backdrops of Norway and white pine and big stands of white birch, popple, oak, and maple. You can see why deer and grouse still abound.

Our tub of a boat was always in dreadful shape, something I knew better than you, for you weren't home much. I'd float around for hours fishing and bailing out the water leaking in. Every spring I'd caulk the tub, but it leaked anyhow. We even packed the cracks with oakum. I thought the word was "yokum," and only when Dad teased me did I get it right. The rowboat would never sink. If it had I was lost, for I couldn't swim. Still can't.

Spring

THIS MORNING, sitting here facing that picture window looking out over Loon Lake, seeing the robins, seeing the pussy willows bursting forth, and snow melted down to a woodsy patch here and there makes the juices in these old veins run. I'm a girl again, and Mom, Aunt Kate, and I are picking arbutus. Like you and Marge earlier, we make corsages complete with sprigs of princess pine and bits of moss. Harry Holperin, owner of the grocery catering to tourists, buys all we have, paying ten cents for white and fifteen for pink. You and Marge hawked the bouquets to tourists getting off at the Chicago Northwestern Station—the train no longer runs. Dad hated some of the shopkeepers, particularly old Richmond of the Rexall Drug Store, who would not buy your flowers; Dad vowed he'd not spend a cent at those stores. These days it's illegal to sell arbutus, it's even against the law to pick them. The air smells washed in balsam and pine. It's as pure as any air outside the Alps. But isn't it weird that the number of local drunks here is probably greater than in any other town of its size in the U.S. of A?

I want to say a bit more about fishing. I felt good bringing home fish, adding to the family larder. In those days, we didn't fillet the fish, so, especially with perch, we had lots of bones to pick. I usually fished with three poles, with night crawlers for bait. I often got up at 5 a.m., had breakfast, and was on the lake by six. At noon, I rested, starting up again at 2 p.m. Large crappies struck as I was oaring. Bluegills and sunfish liked hiding among lily pads. The best fish, small-mouth bass, put up a terrific fight. I read lots of books as I floated around among the lily pads.

Occasionally, I trawled with Aunt Kate, she in her boat, and I in mine. My theory was that if she went ahead, she'd stir up the fish, and I'd catch them. Even at a boat's length off, she'd try brainwashing me.

Among her nuggets was the one I already mentioned: my folks never wanted me. She also introduced me to cigarettes, offering me my first one when I was nine. We had struck a lull when no fish were biting.

Another of my private spots was a swampy island. Here I built a tepee from spindly poplar trees which I bent over and tied with strands of marsh grass. I made myself a bed of ferns, and from the house brought my "Super Woman," "Wonder Woman," "Captain Marvel," and "Batman" comics. No one else knew of this spot. I stayed there many afternoons, and Mom never even missed me.

Thrills on Blueberry Hill

EACH SUMMER we picked berries, lots of them. My favorites were the blueberries, and the huckleberries which were darker and larger and grew in the same patches. Your pail filled pretty fast, but not so with the wild raspberries, which were very squishy. If you ate along while you picked raspberries you ended up with red mush. None of us liked blackberries; they were too seedy and bitter. Yet we picked them in case we ran out of other fruit in the middle of winter. Pin cherries were good for jelly. Remember how we'd fight to taste the first spoonfuls, still hot, thickening? June berries were big and easy to pick. But they tasted like sweetened cardboard, and then the trees died. We went out that summer and found dead branches. I don't think they've ever come back. Some moth laying its eggs probably killed them.

Picking fruit, a family effort, often took us twenty miles from home. Blueberries were best on burned-over land, and news of these patches soon spread. You rushed there before other people marked out claims. We took kettles; lard pails that you fastened to your belt, leaving your hands free for faster picking; and a wash boiler for emptying the pails into.

Some of these trips were scary, for Dad's cars were such heaps that despite his mechanical skills there were always problems. Looking through holes in the rusted floor boards, you could watch the gravel roads speed by under you. On one excursion, the Chevie sedan lost its power; we had to push it up a hill. With our pots, pails, and pans, and our broken down car (this one had a defective frame/spine) we looked like a family of Okies headed West.

Dad, the best picker, after he'd put us where we could fill our buckets, went off alone, returning with as many berries as the rest of us together picked. I was always in charge of Jane, and hated it. We were frightened of bear. They were vicious with cubs in tow. We always returned home exhausted. Mom canned the berries using the hot water method, with jars neatly arranged on wooden slats in a copper boiler.

One July, Dad drove us to the Buckotaban thirty miles north, where he and Everett were cutting wood pulp, earning a quarter a pole. While the rest of us gathered berries, they chopped trees. Mom, you, and Marge were just out of sight, where the berries were thick. I was scared, for I was told to stay near the car baby-sitting Jane. Though hardly more than a babe myself, I could have stayed home with Jane, the two of us alone, but was too scared to, so chose the lesser of two evils, the woods.

Almost from the time Janie was born I was tied to her. Usually I accepted my role without fussing, keeping my real feelings hidden. Jane had a sweet nature. Mom, tired, would say to me: "Jane has to go potty. Take her to the toilet"; "Jane's tired. Put her to bed"; "Nell, take Jane up the road in her buggy"; "Play with Jane in the sand"; "Give Jane your doll, Nell. Yes, I know, she's ripped its head off."

My earliest mistake was that I changed Jane's diaper right after she came home from the hospital. "You're good," said Mom, patting my shoulder. "You'll be my helper." And I was. I took soiled diapers and an old butter knife, and, after shaking the poop into newspaper, scraped each diaper, soaked them overnight in soap and water, and the next morning scrubbed them on a washboard with Proctor and Gamble's yellow bar soap.

On berry-picking excursions, I felt safe as long as Dad wasn't too far off. One afternoon Jane, who was about four, started to fuss. "Shut up," I said. "A bear will eat you. Bears hate girls that cry."

"Lift me up," she said, pointing to the car.

We sat inside with the windows closed, listening for bear.

"Shush," I cautioned. "Was that a bear?"

And there was one, a brown creature sniffing towards us before ambling off into the woods. To this day Jane has not forgiven me for shutting her in the car. "Well," I say, "If you were baby-sitting me and was as afraid to be alone as I was, how would you act?" I'll starve before I pick more berries—those excursions were nightmares.

The Low People on the Totem Pole

THE LOWEST PEOPLE on the local totem pole (if you'll pardon the expression) were Indians who lived as whites. Whites found these reds useful—for it says you aren't lost if there's somebody worse off than you. We saw the Indians as dog-eaters (weren't there always scrawny hounds in their front yards?), and as smelly inferiors. They were also said to eat bear, in those days hardly considered edible by whites. We even said they tossed chipmunks into their stew pots.

The nearest reservation was at Lac du Flambeau, about forty miles west, a wilderness tract of hundreds of acres. Pure fishing streams led to long, winding, isolated rivers. And there were more famous lakes there than anywhere else in the county: Flambeau Lake itself, Fence Lake, and, oh, yes, Sugarbush, White Sand, and Crawling Stone lakes. Then there are all those still unnamed and hard to reach except by four-wheel drive or by long hikes.

The town of Lac du Flambeau, when we were kids, had more birch bark tepees than houses, and the few houses were rickety structures of scrap lumber and tarpaper. One of Roosevelt's WPA programs threw up sturdy yellow privies for the town. These were the best structures there, the best-built. The locals were all on welfare, and Dad drove the relief truck, once a month distributing tins of canned beef, clothing, blankets. You name it: slabs of yellow brick cheese, peanut butter, and lard.

The truck was, as I remember, a clunky Chevrolet with a grinding motor that could die at any moment.

I loved the drive, especially in winter when the roads were just plowed, and the trees were flocked with snow. Partridges would fly up from clumps of white birch and alders, leaving tracks behind in the snow. Deer, feeding in the drifts, appeared. You might set out in crisp sunshine, and before you had gone ten miles, the sky would choke with roiling clouds. The snow would fall in flakes so big you could not see the road. In summer, changes were also dramatic, with cyclones of rain and winds. Wide tornado paths through the forests remained for years.

Dad's welfare truck had a large closed box with back doors through which he climbed for groceries, clothes, and mattresses. Most of the food, except for lard and peanut butter that were wrapped in butcher paper, having been weighed at the warehouse, came in olive-drab tins, all government issue, with "U.S. Department of Agriculture. Surplus Food. Not for Sale" stamped on the sides. Blankets and clothes were labeled with names and addresses. Dad would say how much he loved the Flambeau trips. The Indians were friendlier than the whites he served, giving him fresh coffee and slabs of blueberry pie. Some Flambeau Indians remember him to this day.

We would drive in from the Sundstein District to the Vilas County Court House, where Ann Christian, the mannish former county nurse in charge of welfare programs, checked that her crew had properly loaded Dad's truck. Christian wore her hair in a boyish bob. Her dresses, navy blue, had pockets like those on a man's shirt. Her talk was tough, like her appearance, and she liked Dad's sassing her. To Dad it was a real complement to say she "talked like a man." She thought I was cute, I guess, for she would grab me, hold me to her stubby face and plant kisses. I'd look back at Dad (I was about seven at the time) hoping he'd save me. But there was no cutting "Oatmeal Annie" short.

She was probably ahead of her time. I remember those rumors about her friend Joyce Sparks, a clerk in the County Registrar of Deeds office. The women had lived together for years. Joyce was very feminine. Most people admired their loyalty. Everybody loved (and most were in awe of) "Oatmeal Annie," as she was called.

One Flambeau hovel belonged to "Maggie," an obese woman who sat on three armless chairs pushed together, waiting for Dad to greet her with a cheery "sweetheart." He had a list of items for her, as he had for each family, and he'd check these off, dump them in a cardboard box, and present them.

Another customer was Old Moses. He'd lost an arm in a trapping accident and lived in a shack above the town. He and Dad joshed and laughed. Once Moses gave me a beaded doll, an Indian maid with fringed buckskin skirt and headband.

Before returning to the warehouse, we'd load the truck with comforters made by squaws in the village hall, a project sponsored by the WPA. The government supplied bags of cloth, rolls of cotton batting, needles, thread, scissors, and bindings. These quilts warmed both whites and Indians.

The village of Flambeau today, through community-owned enterprises like an electronics plant, a bingo parlor, a supermarket, and government-built condos and ranch style houses, looks prosperous, though it is, in fact, still very depressed. Old furniture and assorted junk sit heaped in front yards. Deer hides draped over clothes lines rot. Then, obesity is rife—Doritos, sweet rolls, and beer. No matter how positive the Ojibwa image fostered by the tribal museum, few Indians care about their heritage. Some families with brand new houses are said to rip out the wiring, lighting fixtures, and bulbs and barter for booze. While the occasional home is spruced up, most are not, and it is common to see siding ripped off and roofs and sills damaged.

On the Reservation, selling "fire water" was once outlawed. And a white tavern owner who so sold beer to an Indian was heavily fined. Now, that's changed. You'll find bars on all the reservations. Off-reservation joints can't control who buys their booze. Because of all the drunken Indians thrown in there to sober up before returning to the reservation, the County Jail is known as "The Flambeau Hotel."

A scattering of white men, known as "squaw men," marry Indians and even live on the reservation, enjoying tribal hunting and fishing rights. By contrast with the Reservation Indians, those scattered among white communities are pathetic, even tragic.

One squaw-man was George Fetts. Frankie Bauer, a boxer with a national reputation, a Golden Gloves champion, was another. Bauer was a short man whose family owned the largest hotel in town, the Violet Inn. A bank now sits on the site. Bauer once built an airplane from scratch and flew it. After retiring from his Golden Glove days, he returned to Eagle River where he and our cousin Frenchie, Aunt Kate's son, put on exhibition boxing bouts. Eventually, he married a Flambeau woman. His life was sad, for as the result of a fight (on the reservation, I think) which may or may not have been his fault, he killed a man and was sent to Waupun state prison. His last years passed in an alcohol haze. He slept in the local cemetery work-shed, which the City Council ordered sealed, fearing that Bauer might dishonor the corpses. When the weather warmed, he made a hut from cardboard boxes, old linoleum, and plastic. Another of his haunts was a cave under a bridge, deep in a bank. He used some State Park bathrooms, drank from the river, and grilled his food outdoors, much of it animals like deer and squirrel roadkills. According to rumor, he died on the Flambeau Reservation.

One of Bauer's friends was a middle-aged eccentric called "Three Bags" who toted three large plastic trash bags jammed with his worldly goods everywhere. Whenever he bought new items, like soap, he'd always buy triple, one for each bag. He'd been "dim" from childhood when a brother, in a fight, choked him, cutting off oxygen to his brain. Believing he was a railway conductor, he'd spend hours dressed in railroad clothes, standing at the local depot waiting for trains to arrive. He did this long after trains stopped running to the area. One afternoon in late fall he picked up his bags and was last seen heading north towards Land O' Lakes and the Michigan Peninsula.

One Indian family was the Peters clan, living in a clapboard house west of town. We hated being thought their relatives. The irony was rich—for we, like most whites, felt superior to Indians. It was in the air, right? We breathed it. When Mom got mad at us she'd threaten to give us to "those Peters." Dad was always friendly, and when he died in April, 1969, Mrs. Peters, the head of the clan, told me they'd inducted him into the Winnebago tribe. "Now, Nellie," she said, "since he's gone, you'll take his place." I felt proud. My early prejudice rolled like water off a duck's back.

I spoke recently with a daughter of Grace Peters. Grace was in high school with you, Bob. She knew no prejudice growing up. She told me also why her parents did not live on a reservation—they couldn't; they were Winnebagos, not Ojibwas. Winnebagos, moving south from Upper Michigan to work in the saw mill at Phelps, were always considered outsiders by the Flambeaus. As displaced Indians, they never enjoyed the free education, hunting and fishing rights, and welfare programs of the Ojibwas.

My childhood fantasy natives were always modelled after Long-fellow's in "Hiawatha." I've said how I wanted to be an Indian; if gypsies (my other dream folk) turned me down, perhaps a tribe would adopt me.

On our blueberry picking drives to the Buckotaban, at the Deer-skin Flowage Dad would point out the site of the last area Indian conflict. I imagined the braves smeared with war paint, armed with bows and arrows, wearing skins, their oiled tresses bound with leather straps, positioned behind trees, as whites bearing rifles advanced from where a cement bridge now sits. Within minutes, the Indians were either dead or had faded into the woods. Fire weed and Indian pipes spring up there, honoring those noble lives.

The Wish Book

I LOVED the Sears Roebuck catalogue. We all did. You could buy dogs, cats, rabbits, chickens, ducks, turkeys—you could buy anything you wanted. Every spring we ordered white leghorn chicks. Francis Sailer, the mailman, honked his horn to let us know when they arrived from Chicago, and we ran to his car to get the large cardboard boxes punched with air holes. Sears replaced any of the chicks arriv-ing dead. All you did was send in the number. Most, though, made it. Since the weather was still cold, we kept the chicks near the kitchen stove, in a wooden box heated by a kerosene lantern.

I always fantasized over catalogue dolls, knowing we were too poor to order any. I made a cardboard house with tiny furniture and cut out dolls to go inside. A favorite was a teenager with red hair so long you could style it. With scissors I cut out whole families—mother, dad, sisters, and brothers. Patiently, I pasted each figure on cardboard, which I again scissored and mounted on a circular piece of tougher cardboard into which I cut slits. The clothes were a problem, for I had to allow for tabs to pin the dresses and trousers.

Later I bought a "wish book" row boat, fishing poles, and clothes of tough Army cloth with deep pockets, a rain hat with a brim for holding lures, and insulated boots good enough for Alaska. In my dream world, Dad wore clothes like mine, and we fished and hunted, snagging and bagging trophy-worthy game. To be honest, on our actual November deer trails, Dad and I wore layers of underwear, plastic wrapped over our socks, wool sweaters, old flannel shirts, and mackinaw jackets. To display the red marker required by law, we pinned bandannas to our back—all ordered from Sears. When I had to pee, getting those clothes down was awful. I thought my butt would freeze. Men have all the luck!

The catalogue was a poor girl's *Playgirl Magazine*. Models wore skimpy underwear, nighties, and swim suits. My favorite model was black with one of the sweetest smiles I'd ever seen. Not only was she on the cover, but she turned up on several inside pages. I loved slender models best, the ones with bumps in all the right places.

During the summer, in addition to selling arbutus, you, Marge, Everett, and I picked potato bugs (Dad paid us a nickel a can), hoed crops, picked Uncle Pete's corn, and entered animals and vegetables in the County Fair. In August we'd cull the catalogue, balancing the cost of the clothes we'd like for school against the money we had.

The catalogue was also a good door prop, which allowed cool summer air to circulate through the living room and through the whole house. By severely dog-earing the pages, bending them in towards the center, and then standing the book upright, you'd made a shape resembling one of those Iowa corn cribs—you know, ones that look look like a water tower or a smoke house with a sloping roof. Once the catalogue frayed and was no longer useful for propping doors, you hung it on a nail in the privy, where page by page it made for reasonably tidy bottoms.

4

War Dogs and a Pistol in the Night

Cherry Red, Cherry Ripe

IN THE SUMMER of 1944 we moved to Sawyer, near Sturgeon Bay, where Dad worked in the shipyards as a welder, a skill he learned at Rollie's Garage in Eagle River. He moved to Door County six months ahead of us, leaving Everett "head of the family." I still don't know why Mom agreed with Dad that only a male could protect a woman and kids. You, Bob, were already drafted into the Army, and, except for a brief furlough before sailing to Europe, were out of our lives.

Now, since Everett was no longer in school, he had plenty of time to think up torments. His arm-twisting, verbal abuse, and his forcing me to do his chores nearly drove me to suicide. He always got the extra pork chop, chicken leg, or piece of pie. For some reason, he never persecuted Jane—perhaps because she was younger, perhaps because he'd hated me so long. He later got his come-uppance by marrying a shabby woman. Gladys was laughable, for even with a pock-marked complexion and dishwater hair she thought she was sexy enough to sing with a western band. She wore what we used to call "come fuck me" pumps—you know, after the shoes Joan Crawford wore playing cheap women in the movies. Gladys and Everett had a son, and Gladys conned Everett into working two jobs so she could sell her butt to old men. Everett found out, brought divorce proceedings, but had a lawyer so lousy she got the decree and rights to the son—he was never to see the kid again. Later, he tied in with a woman so stupid she could neither read nor tell time. He had better luck with women later on, had a daughter named Dorothy, and eventually became a pure Florida

59

redneck with a construction business and died there of a heart attack. He was only sixty. I guess, you'd say, he paid for his sins. I don't hold too much against him.

Dad left for Sturgeon Bay without having finished our house—which sure didn't make our life any easier. That winter was a nightmare. Simply because the living space was larger than in our old house, keeping warm was a problem. The downstairs kitchen, built into the hill, with rough cement walls, was the warmest spot in the house. While Everett had his own room upstairs, Jane slept with Mom in her bed, and I shared a small downstairs room with Marge, who shortly moved to Wausau to finish high school.

One evening a crisis arose. Mom had baked a lemon pie, my favorite, for my birthday. Beads of crystallized sugar, that tasty "sweat," covered the brown meringue swirls. I can't remember what the main dish was, probably venison steak smothered in onions and tomatoes.

Mom sat at one end of the round oak table, Everett in Dad's place near the sink. I sat to Everett's left. After we had eaten our pie, one wedge remained.

"Mom, can I have it?" I asked.

"No," Everett cut in, grabbing the pie.

"Mom!" I said.

Mom shrugged her shoulders. "He's the boy," she declared, looking away.

Everett gloated as he chewed, his thick glasses smudged. I saw only bits of his irises. I'd never seen such dead eyes. It was hard to read any emotion in them.

Instead of leaving the table, I grabbed the pie, squeezing it through my fingers. Everett tried to spear my hand with a fork, just missing the skin between my thumb and forefinger. He might have nailed it to the table. "You whore!" he yelled, pounding on my shoulder like he thought it was glass.

"Stop," Mom shouted.

I dashed to my bedroom and hooked the door, knowing there was no way I could keep Everett out if he chose to beat his way in. But Mom must have calmed him.

My grabbing the pie was a declaration of independence. At 2 a.m. when I returned to the kitchen, I felt sick and useless. Again in my room, I got my .22 rifle and inserted a bullet, craving the peace I'd have if I shoved the barrel in my mouth and pulled the trigger. During other bad times with Everett I'd considered drowning myself; but Mud Minnow Lake was said to have no bottom, and I feared I'd not be found. Would it matter? I'd be dead, so wouldn't know anyhow that my corpse was shot with formaldehyde, my cheeks stuffed with cotton, my body squeezed into some horrid dress, my hair primped, my lipstick on crazy.

I decided to leave a note for Dad. By the time I'd scribbled it, wearing down the pencil stub, I felt better. I told him how much I loved him, and, as I wrote, I remembered that he was returning from Sturgeon Bay that afternoon. I would ask to go back with him, to keep house.

Most of the next morning I spent in my tepee retreat and out on the lake, in our boat, with my rifle over my knees. Once I reached the center of the lake, I shredded my note to Dad and threw it on the water.

"You're all going back with me to Sturgeon Bay," Dad announced.

We'd make the move piecemeal. Marge would come home from Wausau to help us move. Dad had already rented an orchard farmhouse. Everett and Mom made the first trip, pulling a trailer loaded with our stuff. I don't remember how many trips it took—three, I think; but, finally, after Dad sold our beloved cow to neighbor Frank Kaminski, we piled into the car and drove off, not knowing if we'd ever return.

I was amazed by Lake Superior after all the small lakes scattered around Eagle River. "Look, Nellie," said Dad, pointing towards the horizon. "That's a warship coming in." It looked tiny; yet, when it finally dropped anchor near us, I felt like an ant.

Despite the lure of Superior, I missed our pine trees. Sawyer was all cherry orchards and rolling farmland with a few spindly groves of white birch and sugar maples. The fields were as boring as bleached cow hides. The regional lakes, lacking forests, were lined with summer cottages with rusty screened porches. Gnarled cherry tree trunks were twisted by gnomes out of Grimm's Fairy Tales. Once the cherries ripened, the glow of purple, red, and indigo, was more like a color picture than real life.

We shared our farm house with two other families, one downstairs with a girl my age, another upstairs with a screaming baby. At first I liked the community idea. In time I felt trapped in barbed wire. Worst of all was the outdoor toilet. Each family took turns cleaning and sanitizing. We did, though, have running water. The owner gouged us for rent; he could have afforded indoor plumbing.

One positive: Everett left us. Where he'd gone we didn't know. Let sleeping dogs lie, they say.

No early experiences better trained me for a tough life than those Sawyer days. I was not the power I'd been in the Bohemian school, fighting for the weaker kids, holding my own with the boys. Now, not only did I have to wear dresses to school, but as a kid whose dad worked in the shipyards I was a "shipyard rat." The locals claimed we infected them with chicken pox, measles, and lice. Also, after an I.Q. test, the principal shoved me back to fifth grade. My theory was that according to the law of averages if I randomly answered either A or B on each question, even without reading them, I'd have to pass. I was sure wrong. I got the lowest mark in the whole school. I was a moron.

The fifth-grade teacher, Mrs. Schumack, a short, fat, middle-aged woman with loose gray tresses and a glass barrette, found me offensive. She'd hover, waiting for me to daydream (which I often did). "Pay attention! Do your work and you won't get any more zeros!" She shook me like a dog shaking a cat. Once, to protect myself, I flung my arm out and whacked her fat rear. She expelled me for three days for "hitting a teacher." On returning, I found my bike tires slashed, which meant I had to push the bike home, getting lost. Us "shipyard rats" during recess couldn't play with the "townies" unless we were asked. Well, they asked me! To steal for them. They'd break my arms if I didn't.

One October day, half a dozen boys surrounded me, demanding that I go grab the latest "Superman" and "Captain Marvel" comics from a candy store near school. Alas, the owner caught me. She listened to my tale, decided not to alert the police and instead phoned Dad, who apologized. I was ashamed. But at least I'd proved my mettle to those bullies, who now stopped taunting me.

Walking home from school, I'd follow some railroad tracks past a milk factory, a plant, and a hobo dump for men who would hop freights going West. I liked the cheese plant, for if I timed it right, they gave me a core of cheese pulled from a round when they tested it.

The core was an inch wide and six inches long. My favorite was cheddar.

To the left of the factory, down a slope of saplings and scrub evergreens, was the hobo camp. Cooking fires smoldered under gallon cans suspended by baling wire. Here, for shelters, men tied gunny bags, scraps of cloth, and cardboard to the trees. One man hung up small cloth bags; into each he'd stuck iris and straw flowers, all very homey. He visited the local restaurants, sorting through garbage, finding still edible stuff left on dinner plates by customers. He shared his loot with the other hobos. One afternoon he proudly displayed a dozen pork chops. He was known as "Old Pete." Because Dad had spent his teens with bums, he told me I was in no danger; I could trust these men.

One younger hobo, Mickey, a squat dark man with a ragged beard, from Brooklyn, New York, waved as I followed the railroad tracks carrying my books and lunch pail. One morning he was waiting for me.

"I wanted a good look," he said. I reminded him of his daughter back East. "You're about twelve? That's her age. Elizabeth. Her mom named her after one of them Cat'lic saints. She's devoted, her mom."

"Well," I said, "I can't be late for school."

I liked Mickey, so I often stopped on my way home, sometimes sharing a tin of soup cooked from meat bones collected by Old Pete.

On a mouth harp Mickey played railroad, prison, and sad love songs. Among my favorites were "The Great Speckled-Bird," "If I Had the Wings of an Angel," "The Wabash Cannonball," "City of New Orleans," and "Oh, How I Wanna Go Home." All these songs Dad also played on his violin and squeeze box. The latter, with its keys and flowered bellows, looked like a child's toy compared with those instruments on the Lawrence Welk show. When I gave Mickey a pair of Dad's worn-out work shoes, he was grateful and tossed his own worthless pair into the fire.

One day I found Old Pete's lean-to flat on the ground.

"He died," Mickey said. "From some garbage behind a restaurant. They'd put rat poison on it, I guess." He sighed. "He died on the spot."

During cherry season, farmworkers appeared, seemingly out of the air, as word flew of the Door County harvest. Near the house we rented stood a long, dilapidated wooden barn. In the far half, the owner raised turkeys, a noisy smelly lot, especially in warm weather when the wind blew our way. The other half was arrayed with cots for the itinerant pickers, the single men. Nomad families lived in nearby shacks.

Since we could eat all the fruit we wanted, Mom felt sorry for some of the workers, the young ones without families, so made extra pies. One afternoon I carried two to the barn. The place seemed empty— the men were still in the orchard. I would put the pies down on a wooden crate and leave.

"Hey, girl," said a voice.

A slender blonde youth wearing an unbuttoned blue work shirt had his overalls down around his ankles. He was slightly bearded. "Come on in," he said.

I stepped inside and saw he was fondling his penis. During the seconds I stood there, he jerked himself, flicking his tongue. I had never in my life seen a naked man, and the sight of his big organ sent me high-tailing it for the house. I didn't see then how any man with such a "thing" could walk around in a normal way. Only years later did I understand the mechanics. Back in Sawyer, I would gaze at male crotches, trying to figure, as they say, "the lay of the land."

When eventually I checked with you and Marge, I realized I never fantasized much about my body. I've probably said enough already to show you how much of a retard I was. You tell me, Bob, that you were excited by other males as early as three. You used to run and sit on Charlie Mattek's warm chair right after he left it. Sounds like "instinct," right? Do you like my humor? My point is that you were too little then to choose consciously what you did—God or Apollo, or somebody, had already tapped you. Here's how naive I was, even after I was menstruating: yes, those female models in the Sears Catalogue excited me, but I never drooled over anything below the cheekbones, eyes, and lips—and those sweet sun-lit smiles, I thought, were meant just for me. Though I kissed the pages, masturbation never entered my head. First, I say, you have to have an itch before you can scratch it. And I just never had the itch.

My guess is that most women of my generation felt likewise. Then, my love for Dad, and my mix of female and male urges—one maybe canceled out the other. Also, since I was never a rebel, I pretty much accepted a quiet family role. True, during those ghastly episodes with Everett and later during others with men, sex was never on my mind. To think of that fruit-picker pushed up inside me still makes me cringe. And possibly, in my subconscious, my taste for women's soft bodies grew, as the Bible says, "an cubit." Why make problems? I always say.

Also, my having no fear of hobos related to dreams I had. Their life seemed ideal. When I pretended I was an Indian, or lived with gypsies, I turned to a life of wandering, caring only about myself, an outsider in a money-crazed society. Other women, like-minded, might have become nurses or organized a religious cult. I always felt miserable in church. I never understood, Bob, how you were enough bitten by the religion bug to teach Sunday School with plans to be a Lutheran minister. The Army took that out of you, right? I for one am glad. You thought our family was doomed to Hell (none of us had ever been baptized). So one Sunday you marched us all into church and got us baptized.

The minister was a scary German who believed in universal sin: simply by breaking your mom's amniotic sack you'd broken all Ten Commandments. For forgiveness you were to spend hours on your knees in a closet, pleading with Christ, as your "personal Savior." Each Palm Sunday, in a gutty German-English, wearing black, this man ranted his anti-Boy Scout sermon, damning the Scouts for emphasizing Good Deeds and not Christ's personal forgiveness. Reverend Krubsack, who came from rural Bavaria, did crave the common touch, and he liked very much talking to Dad about crops and animals. Every Easter Sunday he'd blast the Catholics as "idol-worshippers," "graven-image lunatics." Not only were the sermons boring, but I had to wear dresses. I was wretched. The cloth clinging to my hips was like wearing nothing at all. Give me denims any day. To take Holy Communion in Krubsack's church on Friday you visited the parsonage, declaring your intentions. He'd grant some "absolution" and jot your name down. On Sunday your wafer and wine were ready. A dream I had fused Jesus and coconut palms, a dug-out canoe, and a cluster of yammering parrots. I was on a safari and at nightfall I found a settlement, an exact replica of the hobo camp I've described. There were lean-tos of cardboard and gunny bags. But where were the people? Fire under a five-gallon soup tin was blazing. Suddenly, a Chippewa princess in beaded and fringed buckskin dress, her black hair in plaits down both sides of her face, emerged from mist. She walked towards me with her hands extended, wanting me.

Galvanized Metal Poisoning

THE SUMMER of 1945 was the last I spent picking cherries for ten cents a pail, helping the family, and buying my new school clothes for fall. We picked the cherries green for shipping, timing them so they'd reach their destination ripe, or nearly so. All pickers, including entire families, were assigned rows of trees. My companion was a fat, bossy German, Frieda, who wanted Hitler to win the war so I'd be her slave. When I yelled back, she replied, "Shut your mouth, smart-assed kid." She also picked on a scrawny, middle-aged guy who always wore a straw hat filled with holes. She blasted him for being neither in the Army nor in the shipyards.

With ladders we'd climb opposite sides of a tree. Hanging pail belts around our waists, we picked with both hands. Frieda was always mad if I out-picked her. I never had much of a taste for cherries, so was glad when we moved on to apples where we earned fifty cents a bushel. You dropped apples into a gunny bag, similar to horse feed bags flung over your shoulder. They held a bushel, perhaps a bit more.

One noon I hurried home for a bologna sandwich and found Dad in bed. "What's wrong?" I gazed at his pale face. He was still in the overalls and denim shirt he wore to the shipyard. Without answering, he rose up, his chest heaving, and went to the bathroom where he began vomiting real hard.

I ran out the back door to Mom, who was shelling peas. "Mom," I shouted. "Dad's sick."

"He'll be alright," she said. "It comes and goes. He's been poisoned welding. Take him a glass of milk."

He was back in bed with blankets up to his chin, shivering, although the day was hot. His eyes were closed.

"I'm scared," I said.

Mom touched my hand. "He'll fall asleep now. It'll be a couple of hours before his lungs act up again. He says they're on fire."

She led me to the kitchen. "Have this chunk of apple pie. And don't worry. The doctor's coming."

Dad was sick for about a week. His welding job required that he lie on his back seaming overhead galvanized pipes for submarine-chasers. Although he wore a helmet, poisoned fumes seeped in anyway. What he endured was similar to what men in World War I trenches suffered with mustard gas. Two of Mom's brothers had been victims in Belgium, and, though they did survive and come home, their lungs were so burned up they were never able to work. They stayed on the family farm in North Dakota, and only when Roosevelt put through the vets bonus did their lives get better. According to Mom, most vets spent the whole wad on cars or houses, and went back to square one. Her brothers were smart, using it in dribs and drabs, seeing them through to Veterans Administration funerals.

When Dad was finally able to stay out of bed, Mom persuaded him to leave the shipyard. She was sure he'd die. We were ignorant about the welding fumes that caused Dad's cancer; emphysema and the spots on his lung must have started then. He seemed relieved to return home. Everett, who'd seldom been around, returned to help us, as did Marge, who left her restaurant job in Sturgeon Bay. She was ready, too, for home.

Returning was easier than departing. The house was as we left it. Other than woodchuck burrows in the garden, a tunnel below the house (probably made by a skunk), and fly carcasses on window sills, everything was OK. No one had broken in. No one had carted off our woodpiles. Even the hay rick was intact. The empty hen-house, though, was usurped by rats and weasels, a surprising mix.

Within hours, we had the house cleaned. We hung our flimsy mattresses in the sun-washed air and laundered our sheets and blankets. Roaring living room fires soon dried the dank interior. I was so glad to be home.

That fall I returned to the Bohemian School and Mrs. Peale. Here the tables turned: in Sturgeon Bay I was a dummy, and was set back a year. Actually, though, I had read the eighth-grade books, and was ahead in math. Mrs. Peale, bless her, wanted to promote me, but the Superintendent of Schools refused, saying I'd be more mixed up than I already was. The following summer my Uncle Pete had his heart attack. He was only fifty-three. You were in France at the time, in some Army tent camp.

A powerful man, three years older than Dad, Pete always seemed unfriendly, despite his caring for me when I was born in his house. He owned work horses, Bill and Bess, grew two or three times more potatoes, corn, and grain than we did, and cracked a whip over his sons, two legitimate (Jim and Cecil) and one illegitimate (Albert shot himself when he was twenty.) Towards the world, Uncle Pete was stern, and even charged Dad for using his team to plow, drag, and mow our crops. Dad never complained, and seemed to care for his older brother a lot, although Pete kept his distance. For example, they never hunted, fished, drank, or played poker together.

Dad said he never figured out why Pete married Kate, for she was scary, and Dad not only never trusted her, he actually feared her. For she had a history, one Dad told us about, Bob, after both Pete and Kate were dead. Kate's daughter Annie had revealed her story when she thought that with Kate's help Dad might marry her.

Annie's dad, a DeWitt, was an actor in a Shakespeare company playing in American towns. Kate actually once showed me an old sepia picture of him wearing a coat with a big fur collar, holding an ivory-headed cane, and smiling through what was called a Van Dyke beard. Without saying anything, Kate had shoved it back into her "Memory Box" almost as soon as she'd flipped it out.

Once more, when Annie was nine, Kate was pregnant and unmarried. The dad this time was a young roustabout, Vernon Whewell, who had wandered through Muncie (the year must have been 1920) where Kate lived. Annie later told me that her mom would tie her in a high chair in the kitchen while Kate "serviced" men of all shapes and sizes in the bedroom. Annie and Kate were living in a rickety farm house, and Kate would meet young Whewell in the barn loft above where harrows, disks, harvesters, and horses were kept.

Late one afternoon, so Annie said, her mother, carrying rope, took her to the loft. There Kate shredded the dress she was wearing and proceeded to wind the rope about her body, anchoring it to some wooden uprights. Annie pulled on the rope, completing the twists to make it look like Kate had been tied against her will. From a jar, Kate poured chicken blood over her thighs.

"Now," Kate told Annie. "Get the police."

Kate named a local bachelor, Dick Bremerton, a slight, feminine man in his early forties who lived nearby and kept bees, as her rapist. He had "forced" her, Kate claimed, while she was shoving hay into the mangers below. Before she could run, he flung her down, roped her wrists, pasted tape over her mouth, and had his way. Bremerton would have been no match for my sturdy Aunt.

The police, and, later, a jury, believed Kate's story, and Bremerton got twenty years. When he was sentenced, he vowed to kill Kate once he'd served his time. Kate, Annie guessed, liked Whewell the drifter, but knew he'd never settle down; so she spun her cruel hoax. Bremerton died in a prison brawl five years after he was locked up. Kate, nevertheless, persisted in believing Bremerton would keep his promise to kill her.

That morning we heard screams coming from the road. Aunt Kate, barefoot, wearing a flannel nightgown, was hysterical: "Sam! Sam! Sam!"

Pete, with a history of heart trouble, loved a German highly spiced German metwurst. If you had indigestion problems, watch out! Heartburn USA! Although Doc Barney warned Pete against the food, that night, on a Friday shopping trip to town with Kate, Pete ate over a pound of the stuff. Towards morning he awoke doubled in pain. He climbed out of bed and collapsed. Pete was already cold when Dad saw him. All he could do while waiting for the doctor (Everett had gone to town) was to cover him with quilts.

I didn't attend the funeral, but stayed home with Jane, Dad deciding we were too young to go. While I was sorry Uncle Pete died, I don't recall feeling tragic. Even today when I visit his grave, I feel most for my illegitimate cousin Albert who lies near them. His marker draws me. Although he shot himself before I was born, and I've never seen a picture of him, he is, to me, very much alive, a kindred spirit. His headstone seems to have moved two graves over from its original position. Looks like the Cemetery Association is making room for more plots to sell.

So, Bob, after you returned from the Army, in April, 1946, after consulting with Mom and Dad, you took three thousand dollars saved from your Army pay and made a down-payment on a two-story frame house on the west side of Eagle River. Dad sold our forty-acre farm, and Mom now had electricity and running water. You also bought a cemetery plot for the folks, and some clothes for yourself. You enrolled at the University in Madison that fall, on the GI Bill. Oh, there's still enough room in that grave plot for both your ashes and mine, if you can stand being buried that close to me.

My year in eighth grade was smooth. I often made long bike rides through Sundstein to the old home. I flew through the gravel, making the full six-mile loop, ending at the Bohemian School where I'd linger, trying the swings, thinking vaguely about my life. A dream was that I'd become an ace mechanic like Dad and own a repair shop. No woman I knew did such work, and I might just be a success.

I also rode to Lake Seventeen where we used to swim. After tripping through gravedigger Simon's potato field, we reached a rise covered with scrub pines and blueberry shrubs. A few feet below the lake shivered, and was good for swimming until, about fifty yards out, your feet hit muck. I never understood why it was so sandy up close. Despite the hours we'd spend there each summer I never really learned more than a slow dog-paddle, and after five minutes I'd tire of that.

I passed the site of the Sundstein School. The building was moved on rollers three miles to town by the Nazarenes and is still their church. I came to the tumble-down shack where the Three Swedes, brothers, lived and died, one freezing to death on the porch because his brothers were too soused to get up and open the door. Two years later, the remaining brothers were found dead, naked, frozen to one another in their quilts.

On these bike rides I sure missed my dog Waggie. He was a hell of a lot smarter than Shadow. Dad wouldn't let me take him with us to town, saying that was no place to raise a dog used to country living. We gave him to the Howells, the family buying Uncle Pete's farm. Aunt Kate moved to a small wooden house a block down the street from us.

Marge had married a Navy vet, Bob Kauth, and was starting a family. Everett was off chasing women and bad business deals. So, I was at last the king (or queen, if you prefer) of my own castle. Jane, for whom I always felt responsible, and still do today, was a grade-schooler with playmates and a life of her own.

My friends Joanie Adams and Sylvia Dolansky were both boy-crazy. I soon tired of their chatter. Thinking this over, after forty years, my six kids, and my love affairs with men, I feel apologetic for remembering so few old sexual fantasies. What did I miss? If I made up stuff—seductions, orgies—I'd be lying, something I've struggled to avoid here. My memories of that time seem empty. I read a lot, living fantasies that way—you'll still find me with my nose in a book.

They Thought I Shot Her in the Belly

=◦/◦/◦=

AUNT KATE was a short, squat, swarthy person, solid rather than soft. Her upper arms were meaty and her hands small. She'd lock her knees, spread her legs, and protrude her gut like a male wrestler. She always cut her hair straight, using a bowl. Her dresses, short on style and long on wear, she made of cotton, usually with pink and white flowers on dark backgrounds. Totally shapeless at the sides, they were held in by a man's leather belt which she would yank around her belly. She liked cobbler aprons, which had bibs, holes for her arms and head, strings to tie in the back, and flounces at the bottom. These were crazy with rick-rack. She rolled her socks to her ankles and wore men's work shoes. Her honey-colored leather purse, three times the size most women carry, was never out of her sight. She even slept with it under her pillow. Here, she told me, were the sale papers on her farm, notes on what she wanted her family to inherit, and a few pictures of Uncle Pete. Also included were birth certificates, her marriage certificate, and pages ripped from a Bible telling the birth and death dates of her kids and relations.

The purse made me think she was nuts. Night or day, she'd hear steps near her house and would clutch the purse to her bosom. "He said he'd shoot me," she'd mutter once she'd shuffled off to bed. Later I found out who *he* was.

She slapped her ugly living room furniture together herself, hammering pine frames and covering them with imitation leather. There was an arm chair and a decrepit couch seating a person and a half. Footstools she made of tomato juice cans bound together with wire and painted navy blue, her favorite color. The kitchen slop bucket, kept under an open hose leading from the sink, had a colored picture of a smug bull chomping grass and a herd of brown cows clipped from the Milwaukee *Sentinel*. Her house was always too hot, even in winter. While her main heating fuel was oil, she cooked on a wood stove— food tasted best that way. Her living room she kept a constant seventy-five degrees. On my frequent visits I'd prop her front door open until she complained. A musty stink rose from her sweat, an old person's stink. You know, the weak kidney kind. Though she had an indoor toilet, she kept a crockery chamber pot, which she emptied only after she'd used it for a couple of days. She liked using the pot more than she did the indoor plumbing.

Her favorite drink was Kool-Aid. She gave me all the plastic trinkets that came inside the packets. Since we never had Kool-Aid at home (Mom hated the sugar), stopping in to see Kate on hot afternoons was a treat. She'd serve it with a slab of white cake smothered with purple frosting. My favorite meat was fried Spam. Since Spam was cheap, Kate was not as stingy as she was with other foods, including gingersnaps and wafer sugar cookies. If I wanted to please her I'd buy her these—the white, chocolate, and strawberry assortments. She'd eat all the chocolate first. She was messy, so crumbs would stick to the hairs around her mouth. We never got enough Spam, and easily finished off two big cans with slabs of squishy white store bread and potato slabs crisped in a frying pan filled with grease.

Not only was I born in Kate's bed, but our fishing excursions on Mud Minnow Lake, and the hours I spent in her garden (I'd wait until Pete was at work in the saw mill) created what you'd call a *symbiosis*. Dad called her a witch who meddled too much in other people's lives. Only much later, after she died, did I see that I was her familiar—a spook following a witch around, carrying her fleas and sins.

She liked sitting with me on her crummy couch, stroking my hair and running her fingers down my arm. Thank God, she didn't call me "Pussy." She imitated me. If I stood up, she stood up. If I went for a drink of water, so did she. When I went to bed on the couch she'd go to her bed. I often slept over, for Kate was afraid of being alone. I'd usually conk out and fall asleep in my bra and panties. In the middle of the night, she'd come out and watch me sleep. "You sure sleep sound," she'd say. "I sat there over an hour. You didn't even hear me." I didn't then see how crazy she was.

You may think it odd (and I guess I do, too) why I preferred her company to that of girls my age. Most of them "walked" in the park, not to admire the mallards but to cruise boys. Their favorite area was a cinder parking lot by a tacky tennis court, just past the Chicago Northwestern Station (now defunct) you see right after you enter town. The popular girls had it all over me. It took years before I, too, switched off that ugly duckling feeling.

The tragedy happened on the first Friday of September, 1947. I was fifteen and about to start high school. I had gone to the Vilas Theater to see "Dick Tracy: Scarface," and reached Kate's at 9:30. She was cheerful, and we had our usual Spam, cake, and cherry Kool-Aid. Since the movie was scary, I had trouble falling asleep.

Shortly after midnight I heard a thud, or was it a fire-cracker? I threw back my quilts and hurried to Kate's bedroom. From the street light falling through the window I saw her face; she'd pushed her hair back.

"I'm shot!" she said, facing me.

"What?" I exclaimed, switching on the overhead light, hurrying to her bedside.

"Somebody was in the window." She tried to sit up. "A man. I saw his shape."

"You've had a bad dream," I said. "I had one, too."

She started to cry. She was helpless lying there in her flannel night gown.

"Don't worry," I said. "I'll help get you to the folks." We lived less than two blocks away. "If you feel tired, I'll carry you."

When I thrust my arm under her back, preparing to lift her into her house coat, I felt something warm and sticky. "You're hurt," I exclaimed. The blood, oozing, felt like pee. The smell was of gun metal, sickening.

"I'll go fetch Dad," I said.

She was moaning: "Oh, I'll die. I'm shot. Don't let me die."

"I'll get Dad," I repeated, not thinking the killer might still be in the house. I threw on my pullover and jeans.

She clutched my coat. "Get me some water," she groaned.

"Here," I said, returning from the bathroom. From her bed she had a clear view into the darkened kitchen, and she never shut her door. "Moisten your lips with this cloth. Suck on it until I get back with Dad." You shouldn't drink liquids when you're shot.

When I flicked on the kitchen light I noticed rifled drawers. Also, the back screen door was slashed. As I turned to leave, my foot struck something! A pistol! I picked it up and I laid it on the chair next to Kate's bed. Since Kate was good with guns (she was even better than Uncle Pete) she'd have the gun handy if the attacker returned. Had he thrown the weapon towards my couch? It didn't make sense.

That block and a half took forever. Sumac shrubs wiggled, hiding a killer. The dim street light only made the shadows scarier. Our house, with the big blue spruce in the front yard, was dark. Fortunately, since we never locked the door, I didn't have to fumble for a key. I don't think I could have coped.

Dad was snoring, with Mom lying beside him. I shook him awake. "Dad. Dad. Aunt Kate's shot. She's dying. Hurry."

Back at Kate's (Mom called the sheriff) Dad said there was nothing we could do until the doctor and the ambulance came. He snooped through the house and then told me to wash the blood from my hands. Kate all this while was surprisingly quiet.

When Sheriff "Red" Hebert arrived, Kate started moaning: "Nell, Nell, why did you shoot me? Why?"

I was flabbergasted. Why would she accuse me, her fifteen-year old niece? With her nightie up around her waist, the small clean bullet-hole showing in her belly, she looked like a ventriloquist's doll. She wasn't my Aunt.

Hebert quieted her. When the ambulance came, they wrapped her in blankets, carried her out of the house, and drove her to St. Mary's hospital in Rhinelander. Hebert had sense enough to bring in a ballistics expert. The bullet tore up her lower colon some, but not enough poop leaked out to case infection; or, more likely, the doctor cleaned her out in time. They retrieved the bullet.

Hebert, a fishing guide with no crime experience, elected sheriff only that spring, clumsily interrogated me. He scribbled notes on a legal pad. I had no idea what was in his mind. I even thought the worst was over—what could I say? Since he and Dad were friends, I anticipated no hassles. Soon Hebert's questions turned into a nightmare, leaving me trembling and crying. For the next three days, in one-hour blocks of time, he questioned me. Obviously, to him, a good investigator asked the same dumb things over and over, finally wearing his "suspect" down. Imagine yourself at age fifteen. How would you behave? I was suspected, for not only would my finger prints be on the gun, which Hebert so far hadn't found, but my story of putting the weapon by Kate's bed didn't jibe with the fact the gun was not there. What had Kate done with it during those minutes when I went for Dad?

Though Hebert had no motive for me, apart from an accident, Dad got nowhere trying to convince him I was innocent. "Well, Sam," Hebert said coldly, "you don't know everything that goes on in a kid's mind." I would be charged for attempted murder.

"Will she have to be locked up?" Dad meekly asked.

"No, we don't have room in the jail for kids her age."

The next morning, Hebert found the gun stuck inside a leather holster deep in Kate's wood pile. The initials "SB" were stamped on the holster flap. The ballistic expert, though, was the one who finally cleared me, for he'd examined Kate in the hospital, before they cleaned her up. "This gets you off, Nellie," Hebert said, touching my shoulder. "She must've shot herself. The powder burn on her belly shows the bullet was fired at an angle suggesting she did it." He sounded very smug, as though he and not the expert had figured this one out.

They traced Kate's revolver to Stan Busher, her son-in-law, whom she hated. His wife, Kate's daughter Grace, though not yet twenty, was a lush with two boys still in diapers, each by different fathers, neither by Busher. One dad was the chief local boozer, Axel Castleburg, a frequenter of Sam's Tavern where Grace, leaving the infants home, often danced. Gossip says she liked doing it behind the upright piano.

As a boy, Busher had shot and killed an older brother in a hunting accident. Maybe by putting up with Grace's shenanigans, even, in his way, loving her, he was paying for his boyhood "crime." For over six years he supported Grace and her kids. She'd nag him to the breaking point, and later appear at Kate's door with black eyes. Kate would storm off to confront Busher who, drunk, sneered, called her filthy names, and slammed the door in her face. In time, when Busher had left Grace and the County had committed her four kids to foster folks, Annie took them in, in pairs, raised one set, then brought in the other two. Years later, Busher was clobbered with a skillet by a drunk and today is a vegetable in a veterans' home near Milwaukee.

Obviously, Busher's fingerprints were on the gun—as were mine; and so were Kate's. Hebert now believed that Kate hated Busher so much she tried to trap him. It didn't work, for Busher produced a tight alibi. Hebert closed the case. Kate never did admit she'd shot herself. Until she died in her eighties, alone in the nursing home, still clutching her purse, she never told anyone the truth.

Within days, her daughter Florence drove her back to her house. At school I was a celebrity; and, I must say, I didn't mind. For once in my life, my iceberg poked up high above the others. Some kids refused to believe I'd not actually pulled the trigger.

This photo was taken by Sam Peters during the summer of 1933, when I was a year old. Behind us (*from left to right*: Marge, Everett in overalls, Mom, me on Mom's lap, and Bob shielding his eyes) is the kitchen portion of the house with its scrap lumber exterior, and very homemade screen door and window sills.

This shot, taken by Mom in 1939, was meant to show the array of instruments Dad played by ear rather than suggest our individual musical skills. Only Bob was adept enough at the guitar to play with Dad in public.

How our log and tar-paper house looked around the spring of 1941. Bob is in his band uniform. The lumber scattered in the foreground was used by Dad to build a bedroom and kitchen behind the original house.

Here I am with sisters Marjorie and Janie and my beloved Dad, on our return from Lutheran church services. Dad's suit, the only one he ever owned, was a heavy serge affair supplied by the county welfare department. Mom snapped the picture around 1940.

Dad and Mom during the Sawyer shipbuilding days, in front of our house. Dad is dressed to go to work.

Aunt Katie Katherine Peters some dozen years before she shot herself. As her dress shows, she had no sense of fashion, and the pile of logs waiting to be sawed into firewood was very much a part of her ambience.

My high school graduation picture. I like it, except for the ugly mass of red hair living a life of its own on the side of my head.

Here I am as a WAC. I've always liked this picture.

Here I am with the twins in my folks' yard in Eagle River. It's hard to tell David Michael and Michael David apart, right?

Kate soon moved a couple of miles from town to live with her daughter Florence, her husband Carl, and his mother Isabel, an educated woman whose husband had clerked for years in the local bank. Carl drove a taxi, and made a good living, especially in the tourist summer season. Florence, like Kate, was a mannish woman who raised chickens, geese, and rabbits, and chopped down trees. She was herself barren. The two old mothers Kate and Isabel fought all the time. Kate won, for Isabel, seventy-five, died within the year. Later that summer, felling Norway pines in order to clear ground for rabbit hutches, Florence dropped a tree against some high line wires and was electrocuted. The power in the area had to be turned off before her charred body could be removed.

Kate then moved in with Annie and her brood. Annie's husband Tom, the former sailor, now in Argentina, sent checks, visited only every three years, just long enough to impregnate Annie before returning to South America. Years later Annie learned that he had an Argentinian family. Kate, as baby sitter, freed Annie to work as a cook in local restaurants. She was famous for her navy bean soup. Kate, Annie found, piled caches of food in her room, stolen from Annie. When Annie bought new underwear for herself, it would turn up missing; she found later that Kate had given it to Grace, now a total lush. One morning, Annie heard a noise, went to check the kids, and found Kate with a pillow over baby Tommy's head. At this point, Annie drove her mother, and purse, to the local nursing home where eventually she died.

How to explain the impact on me of Kate's shooting? Like most big things in life, this one's still buried, like loon shit piled up over years in a lake. You've dug for connections, Bob, and no matter how frank I am, you really can't get past what would make this book sound more like a novel than a woman's true life story. I'm frustrated reliving Kate's shooting. Why she tried to frame me still boggles my mind.

No, her shooting doesn't explain my need for people. Yesterday, when I tried to nap, there were half a dozen phone calls—no lie. Two were from my kids—from Marilyn, and from Shannon in Upper Michigan wanting to see you. Her crippled ten-year-old may have to lose his legs and be fit with false ones. Other calls came from the commander of the Legion Post who wanted advice from me, the former commander. Yes, my kids drop by almost daily, and my youngest, Gus, lives here, treating me more like an equal than a mom. He vows he'll get his act together.

After Kate's shooting, some of my short supply of self-reliance did turn to smoke. I admit it. Therapy, you say, might bring this out? It's too damned late, Bob. I've turned sixty. You should know better. Who needs it? And back in 1946, there were no support agencies. Today, after such a mess, I'd see several county and state therapists, free. Back then, they left you on your own, to sink or swim. Was it fair? Who knows?

My anger at Kate for betraying me makes sense. I said earlier that I was her "familiar," the witch's pal. If witches end up destroying their cats, toads, imps, or whatever, then the parallel fits. Did she draw me to her, counting on my affection, just to wreck me? I was pissed over what she did and avoided her for years, seeing her only with other people. Neither of us ever spoke of the episode. She sold her house and, after paying Annie half of the proceeds for her life-time "room and board," she kept the rest of the cash in her purse. I like to think that when she died her survivors emptied the damn thing, settled the Old Folks' Home bill, and threw the purse in the coffin with her, placing it by her feet. I can see her on her way to Hell trying to wriggle the damned thing up into her arms. She'd never even trust the Devil!

One message I got loud and clear was that if you get too close to some people they can burn you to a crisp. Yet, I've always been friendly, maybe too much so, which led in my middle years to a period of boozing past the safety-point. I'd always get super-happy drunk. I've always been generous with hugs and kisses, as my kids and grandkids know. And the dudes I've had affairs with, and my one disaster with a woman, all liked my snuggling. In general, I get on best with men, and always have. Women still threaten me; I'm not petite and cute enough for most of 'em. But let's not go any deeper into that right now, for you'll tie it all to my "fixation" on Dad. With men I share talk, filled with boasting, without the jealousy that keeps me from getting too near to women. I was never much of a flirt, wrist-flasher, or boobies-bouncer. It's the difference, I guess, between bear liver and calf liver. One gives you the balls, so to speak, for surviving a terrible life; the other doesn't even come close. Give me bear liver any time! The big bass over the fingerling. As my dad used to say: "If you can't dazzle 'em with brains, baffle 'em with bullshit."

Also, no matter what crap rains down you have to get on with your life. This is my philosophy. Like a dog burying a bone, you throw an experience into a grave and somewhere up the road you dig it up again. If you, Bob, weren't here this spring I'd probably never plunge my paws in the dirt, digging up these rotten bones. Yes, Kate sure scared me. I still dream of that night, and, as I'm about to find the gun I wake and get up long enough to shake the dream back into the wool of the past where it belongs. So, you can see why I'm not too happy with you for what you're doing. Somebody lookin' through the window might guess some sado-masochism, or whatever it's called, is going on. What do you think of them apples, brother?

5

County Fair, Cadavers, and Romance

⟨◦/◦/◦⟩

County Fairs

⟨◦/◦/◦⟩

I'M CHILLY sitting here with all the garage crap spilled behind me—and I'm thinking about August when it's warm, and the country fair. You can see that my business today is awful slow—it's been one hell of a rainy week. Folks won't stir far from their space heaters. Not many men out on the lakes. Think positive, Nellie, I say. If I displayed my stuff better, the way they do at the fairs—all the baked and canned goods, FHA needlework, flower arrangements, birdhouses crafted from wood. . . . If I had shelves on wheels that would slide across the lawn to the street, with items for sale neatly arranged, that might help. I'd clean up Shadow's poop first, for she does favor that spot by the mailbox. Say, where is that critter? She was here a minute ago. *Shadow! Shadow!* I'm going to have a lung hemorrhage yelling at her. You have to put the fear of God in pets, then love 'em hard. Here she comes. Good dog, Shadow. *Now, lay down!*

The fairs were sure special, weren't they? We all pitched in, the whole family, entering sewing, animals, chickens. For this next one I'm making quilts for my grand kids. I'm working on pieced quilts for you and Paul. He, Paul, sure deserves one, after all the thinking he's put into this book. It's like he's been writing it with us. I think you'll use the quilts, though it doesn't get as cold in California as it does here. As Dad used to say, some of these thirty-below-zero nights would freeze the balls off a brass monkey.

The Fair's been held in the same spot west of town ever since I can remember, down by the river. The gray exhibition buildings and the grandstand. . . . By noon on Friday the carnival is set up, and all the exhibits are judged. Of our three big public celebrations—Memorial Day, the Fourth, and the County Fair—I looked forward most to the fair. It's always fun. Simply by stepping onto the grassy grounds you whiff something animal, "snaky," or sexy. Tent canvas stink blends with cut grass smelling like garter snakes. And then there's always the smell of cotton candy and caramel corn. I used to go wild when I was a kid. The colored lights were amazing, after those in Eagle River where anemic neon glowed from Mint's Bar, Bandow's Tavern, and a Woolworth's store. That was about it. The ferris wheel was painted with birds of paradise. You didn't notice how beat-up the seats were. The gilt and silver merry-go-round always framed a beach scene with palm trees, a girl in a sarong wiggling her butt in a coconut grove, roaring lions, and a poster of adorable Betty Boop.

The Shriners and the Elks ran beer booths. Attractive high school girls, and some older women, ogled the carnies and roustabouts who cranked and ran the engines. There was a scary Tilt-A-Whirl.

Gossips said that on those August weekends more local girls lost their virginity than on any other weekend of the year. My friend Mabel DeVerney claimed she could smell sex, the smell of Guernseys in heat. She had some imagination! A big deal was the baseball game between town whites and the Lac du Flambeau Indians. Seeing the Indians drunk, and their squaws crowding the diamond, pulling hair and screeching, was both scary and fun. Games were called before the final innings.

As a family we did good on the prizes, for animals, fowl, needle work, canned food, bakery goods, and produce—and for school work, creative writing, art, and projects sponsored by the Scouts, the 4H, and the Future Farmers of America. Nearly every entry won a ribbon, and though the cash prizes were small, they helped us buy school clothes. Even burnt cakes and pies and crummy crocheted doilies won third-place ribbons.

Remember that white sow and eight piglets? You were with me when this henna-rinsed, middle-aged Chicago woman with big orange earrings, drunk, flopped her tits against the planks, grabbed up a piglet, and started kissing it on the lips. Both sow and piglet squealed, and when the mother flung herself against the boards, throwing her feet up towards the woman, the piglet squirmed back into the pen; but not before she peed all down the front of the woman's blouse. Served her right.

Our chickens always won prizes. We entered them as white leghorns, although they actually were a mix of leghorn and ancona,
a dark breed. The night before the fair, we'd yank out the black
feathers—these would have shown the judges that our birds were not
pure leghorns. We always fooled 'em. Was that cheating?

Then the sideshows. I never had the nerve to watch a geek woman
bite off a chicken's head. I did see a fat man and a woman with a
beard. You used to tell me about John Wilkes Booth's corpse, all
parched, looking like smoked salmon. The barker tapped Booth's
femur with a cane, showing where the bone broke when Booth
jumped down from Lincoln's theater box shouting that stuff in Latin.
Must have been a hoax, for it never reappeared at future fairs. You
weren't lying to me, were you?

Around and Around We Go

IN A MEMORY (I'm seven) the folks force Marge to take me to the
fair. She has a date with Hiram Ewald. We've hardly reached the ferris
wheel when she dumps me into a swinging seat. I assume she's going to
ride with me; but she has other plans. The attendant fixes the bar and
I start moving. I'm not scared, but I am soon bored. Marge and Hiram
pay for ten continuous rides. I finally spot them in Hiram's car just
past the sideshow tent where freaks are exhibited. They seem to be
just sitting there side by side, not even smooching. They don't hear
my shout. I don't blame Marge for wanting her privacy, for I often felt
trapped when I had Janie in tow. My guess is that Hiram worshipped
Marge, but that she didn't care much for him. The ferris wheel opera-
tor smiles, slows the car as though I'll stop, but keeps me spinning. I
start yelling, forcing the guy to let me off.

I really enjoyed the free grandstand acts. Among them were tra-
peze artists, magicians, dogs in polka-dot collars and silly hats, and
local musicians. You, Dad, and Charlie Mattek played your country-
western numbers. Dad was on fiddle, accordion, and mandolin. You
strummed a few guitar chords. You never looked like you enjoyed it.
Charlie, a man women loved despite his clumped right leg—he wore a

foot-high lift under his right shoe, plus a leg brace—not only sang but strummed a mean guitar, with or without the capo. You three played, as I recall, most Saturday nights at Sam Capich's log tavern, a popular spot just past the cemetery. Oh, I fell in love with Charlie. Join the line!

Among the performers was Helen Tarkington, who imitated "Patsy Montana," the national Grand Ole Opry star. Her boyfriend Norm Jason aped Pat Buttram. Helen, with long black hair, looked petite in a white peasant blouse, black square-dance skirt, white cowboy boots, and a western hat. She was peppy, and with her nice voice had a big following. You were smitten with her, right? Jealous of Norm Jason? You were in the same grade at school. Helen's theme song was also Montana's, "Winkin' at Me."

At other fairs, I would linger around the carnies, craving to join them and run off. Yes, they were good physical specimens, especially the men with their hard bodies crammed into tight jeans, with tattoos of naked mermaids, anchors, roses, and lilies all down their arms. Some of the women had those rear-end spreads we call "the Wisconsin Triangle," the enormous asses. Other gals, though, were cute and sexy. The carnie men all flirted with local girls. I don't think there was a homo among them. The carny women's hard lives scribbled disaster messages all over them too early. Yet enough were curvy and sexy to whet my appetite. I would throw my dimes down and toss rings or whatever, hoping to start a conversation with a carnie girl. Before my leg went bad on me (from poor work conditions in the battery plant, I've always believed), I promised myself I'd that buy that once-in-a-lifetime Harley Davidson I mentioned before, that leather outfit, and ride to California to see Paul and you, stopping at lots of carnivals and circuses, finding true love and happiness. What a dream! To this day I flirt with waitresses in trucker cafes who are pretty with swept-back no-nonsense hair-dos and crisp, frilly aprons and pencils stuck behind their ears.

On the last night of one of the fairs, I was standing where men swing mallets to ring a bell by slamming a post like one of those that ships tie up to. Dad won cigars here. That night I actually wore a dress, believe it or not, a light blue one with a pleated skirt Mom had sewn for my junior year when I might be going to the prom. The top was short-sleeved with a pocket, similar to one on a man's shirt. And my hair looked good, for Mom had treated me to a permanent, the second I'd ever had, at Verna's, where she, Mom, always got her monthly rinse and set.

Standing there, with the merry-go-round music pulsing, the lights playing all over the grass, and people talking and laughing, I felt a touch, and when I turned, there was Hurley Remington smiling, inviting me up in the ferris wheel.

Hurley, six years older than I, was Helen Tarkington's cousin, the Patsy Montana singer. He worked in Chicago, and on most weekends drove the five hours to see his Mom.

"I like you, Nell," he said, as we entered the ferris wheel.

Sylvia Dolansky had been dating him, so I wondered why he was after me. "You're going with Sylvia, right?"

"Was," he replied. "*Was* going with her."

Hurley was stocky, slightly hunched, and had protruding ears. In one of my joking moods I saw his ears as mushrooms, you know, the sort you pick, dry, and use for lighting firecrackers: punk. He did have nice eyes—chocolate with a hint of purple. Bristly eyebrows.

Afterwards, he drove me home, gave me a safe kiss, and said he'd be back the next weekend.

Mamma's Boy

THE REMINGTON'S large oak dining table seated a dozen people. Overhead was a pull-down lamp shaped like a wagon wheel, with four bulbs. Nora Remington was proud of her Avon perfume bottles arranged on shelves across the room. There were "bell girls," figures in glass and plastic with voluminous skirts. Some glass cars, once filled with men's shaving lotion, sat beside silver deer, rabbits, and bear rearing up on their hind legs. She'd hoped to get all the heads of the U.S. Presidents, but knew she couldn't. She did have fifteen, including a rare Franklin Pierce. Paper doilies made dusting the shelves easy; she could simply grab a doily, give the objects a shake, and then rearrange the shelves.

Nora's taste was all over the room. School photos of her eight kids stared from metal frames. Her coffee table, built by Hurley in a shop class, of light birch, joined at right angles, with one section atop the other. In front of her picture window were an asparagus fern and a Christmas cactus which, she claimed, loved coffee grounds. Her pride and joy, though, were African violets in foil-covered pots. The best one was a blue so intense it looked purple.

Nora was short, with a pinched face, and wore thick glasses with wire rims. Since her house was always neat, you'd expect her glasses to be the same; but they weren't. If you caught the light shining just right, you'd wonder how she saw anything, they were so filthy. And the frames, twisted, gave you the feeling she was scrutinizing you, with one of her irises lower than the other. Her short black hair, coarse, barely covered her big ears. She still had a Missouri twang, and if you dressed her right, complete with corncob pipe, she'd make a perfect Mammy Yokum. For so tiny a person she had an almost male voice, one she used to control her husband Bill, Hurley, and the other kids. She didn't invite you to like her.

One Sunday, after Hurley introduced me, Nora shook my hand, looked crabby, wiped her hands on her red checked apron and muttered: "We'll eat in ten minutes." She returned to the kitchen where I heard her rattling pans and running water. I wanted to make a good impression. I could have worn a dress, I suppose, but Hurley, I thought, liked my jeans, shirt, and the green wind-breaker.

Fortunately, Sally, Hurley's sister, who was in my year at school, was there with her date, Fred Swan. Fred, a dozen years older than Sally, ran a Texaco station. Two younger sisters were also present.

Hurley's dad sensed I was uneasy, so led me to the dining room where we seated ourselves around the table. The main dish was a juicy slab of roast beef with mashed potatoes, string beans, coffee, and apple pie. No one ate until Nora picked up her water glass and signalled the start of the meal. I sat between Hurley and Sally, out of Mrs. Remington's direct line of sight. After she'd passed Hurley his pie—she'd served it on his favorite plate, one with a Dutch windmill in blue—she suddenly said to me, using a snide tone: "Victoria Dolansky also liked apple." I felt three inches tall. Hurley had dated Victoria for over two years.

After dinner Hurley and I toured the barns, gardens, and fields. A buck, doe, and a fawn had moved in to feed with some Holstein heifers in an alfalfa pasture. By easing forward, then standing still, we got close before the buck snorted, flashed a white scut, and leaped through the trees.

"Deer are all over," Hurley said. "We eat plenty of venison."

"I'd like to raise a fawn," I said.

He laughed. "Bambi?"

"You shit!" I exclaimed. "If it was a buck I'd call it Hurley."

He looked at his watch. "We'd better get to that movie." Three Lakes was ten miles away.

Once inside the house, Hurley kissed his mom. "Won't be too late," he promised.

"Well," she said, "you have to get up early for Chicago." She knew he'd disappoint her. Hurley gave a shy smile and started out the door, drawing me after him. His mother didn't look up.

"What did happen?" I asked. "With Victoria, I mean. She's my friend, too, you know." I'd assumed they would marry.

"Oh. It's simple," Hurley said. "We just broke up."

"I'm no dummy, Hurley. I know that." I believed Hurley that it was over. I'd heard that Victoria was pregnant by a Chicago tourist.

On our dates, apart from the occasional movie, we either played cards with his folks or with mine. We were seldom alone; the five-hour trip from Chicago wore him out, and he'd feel guilty if his mom thought he'd come to see me and not her. This wimp never pushed me for sex, although we did a lot of serious petting, the kind that moistens your panties.

He was the first man I ever kissed romantically. From reading novels I'd expected Sheer Bliss when a man made love to you. I was never a very good necker, I admit it. All you did was pucker your lips and let the juices flow. I was disgusted when Hurley stuck his tongue in my mouth. Was he trying to count my teeth? Was I a horse he was buying? "Don't," I said. It was cold in his car. One novel advised turning your lips back, exposing their satiny inner lips, for a real thrill. Be blowfish sucking love-juice air up from each other's lungs. Ugh!

Because I was dating Hurley the other girls thought I really liked men. I had lots of red hair, those breasts that people joked about, a nice smile, and lively (so I was told) eyes. Any guy would be proud of me, Hurley said. My parents liked Hurley, and he liked them. I rarely felt much deep romantic stuff, few sexy impulses from a virginal wood, so to speak, where I wanted to yank off his clothes. On his bi-weekly visits, I liked seeing him drive up. We'd soon settle into our soft-ball routine, or, to use another image, we were like friendly tetras lolling inside a tepid aquarium. Though we smooched a lot, we were like brother and sister, two safety matches capable of being struck and lighted but never are. Our affair saved Hurley's face over being duped by Victoria. Hurley, never possessive, was always a bit smug, as middle-aged men often are. I'd joke about his socks, those rayon kind with the cheap ribbing that old men (or so it seems to me) wear. For dressing up, he liked conventional oxfords with holes in the wing tips, which he bought at Frankel's store in Eagle River, boasting how he'd "jewed old Frankel down." Hurley got the short end; for Moses Frankel knew that anti-Semitic Eagle Riverites would barter. He'd jack up the prices in the first place and then come down; the locals thought they had a bargain. On my slide rule, on a hormone scale of ten, Hurley pulled a big fat one.

After a few months, he sensed I was getting bored, for on a Christmas trip he drove to our house, came inside, and plopped down in an old cherry-wood rocker opposite Dad. We'd trimmed our tree with glass ornaments. Some were Mom's favorites from her child-hood—glass vials, angels, Santas, and colored bells. Jane had made chains of colored paper, and images of Santa cut from construction paper and hung with paper clips. Although only four days remained till Christmas, I had not bought Hurley a gift other than an eight-by-eleven enlargement, in a frame, of my school photograph. I didn't know if he'd want it or not, especially after I said I wanted to break off with him.

"You look sad," he said, pulling me to his lap. I had on my blue dress, since we'd had plans for a dance at the Town Hall.

I caught Dad's smile when Hurley tried to kiss me. I must have been tense, for I got up, colored, then sat back down, tousling Hurley's brown hair. From his pocket he drew forth a black box about an inch square with a humped top. "Here, Nell. It's for you." Inside was a silver engage-ment ring with a small diamond. He slipped the ring on my finger. The next week, the local newspaper published our announcement.

Hurley's plans numbed me; not that I felt, as I've said, much love. We'd neither of us billed and cooed sweet nothings. As for sex, he said we should wait for marriage—and this suited me just fine.

As he described our future, I saw the grim face of his mother and heard her voice, like a ventriloquist's. After the Lutheran Church ceremony, forgoing a honeymoon, we'd drive to his Chicago apartment. There, amidst furniture chosen by him, I would unpack my clothes, lose my virginity, and find a job. I felt like chattel, I think that's the word. Old-fashioned, I thought he should support me. Without any job training, all I could hope for was an assembly-line job soldering the innards of radios, hi-fi sets, and such. Though I was certainly no *feminist*, I refused to be exploited. A partnership was something Hurley couldn't see. If we married I'd have my work cut out. Could I reform him? I might first have to drop arsenic in his mom's coffee.

Street Dance

THAT SPRING, the town put on dances, blocking off Main Street and hiring a country band. Charlie Mattek, our family friend (though by now he'd divorced Dad's cousin Evelyn), had formed his own trio, for which he was the guitarist and lead singer. Dad had given up playing in public, and you, Bob, no longer interested, were off in the Army and at the University of Wisconsin, to exotic places. Though crippled, with a twisted leg and a shoe-riser, Charlie charmed everybody, male and female. Even as a child, I craved to be near him. He told Hurley: "You might be marrying my girl, but I was the first man who ever slept with her."

And that was true, for, during a blizzard, he and Evelyn weren't able to reach their own house a mile away, and so stayed over night. I was six. They piled into bed with me. Evelyn slept in the middle.

At the end of the closed street, on bales of hay piled onto a wagon, Charlie played, accompanied by Buff Strang on sax and Ron Dunham on accordion. Charlie would extend his braced leg in a curve so that the sole of his black shoe shone. A pair of mikes, throwing feed-back, were fussed over by Francis X. Johns, the fat photographer and camera-shop owner, who owned the set-up. The music jangled, the sax off key, the accordion lagging behind Charlie's guitar riffs.

A crowd pleaser was "Wipe-Out," where the tempo moved to a

frenzy then shifted key, stopping before picking up again. There were three dancers. The middle dancer, usually a male, swung in patterns, taking the arms of the other dancers. The music originated with a waltz followed by figure eights before the musicians segued into a schottische.

Charlie's specialties were the tunes he used to play with you and Dad: "Under the Double Eagle," "San Antonio Rose," "Listen To the Mocking-bird," "The Wabash Cannonball," "The Beer-Barrel Polka," "Blue Eyes," and "The Wreck of the Old Ninety-Seven."

One night Charlie arrived for the dance and found he'd forgotten to bring the shirt he usually wore, a denim with sequined pockets and a silver lariat across the shoulders. He asked me if I had a western shirt that would fit. "Sure," I said, and rushed home, pulled it from a drawer, and hurried back. Woolen, it was dyed deep blue with flowered quilt pieces set as panels down the front.

"Perfect," he said. "Thanks."

I helped him into it, buttoning the shirt, leaving the collar open. When I took the garment home I didn't wash it for weeks.

Bill Griffin

BILL GRIFFIN resembled Montgomery Clift, before his car accident, and had some of the same reserve. He had a foul reputation; he came across as shy, yet women ached to smother him. There was much Irish charm, a sculpted face with thin lips, and a dimpled chin. If I make him sound perfect, he sure looked that way. He combed his brown hair in a pompadour. His eyebrows, like his other features, were just right, neither too thick or too thin. He never wore overalls, jeans, or those felt pants local men wear during real cold weather. He always wore pressed gabardines and a broadcloth shirt with a sleeveless pullover. I would tease him about how the gabardines hugged his butt, the part of him that excited me more than the others. I saw it bare only once, in the back seat of his car in moonlight. His coats and jackets were classy. My favorite was padded, with deep pockets, like ones game-hunters wear. His family roots were mysterious, and still are. His granddad told me his last name was Hanley. His dad was a barber who impregnated the daughter of the Eagle River undertaker old P. J. Griffin. All locals, sooner or later, passed through Griffin's hands, prepared through his cosmetology for the next world. Only Doc Barney saw more citizens naked.

P. J.'s daughter left town, returning a few months later with a Baby Bill. P. J. adopted the kid. Bill claimed that despite legal ties to the Griffins he was always a "floater." My guess is that he never knew his real dad. To the world, his mother was his "sister"—that was the part she played. I've cared a lot about this, for reasons I'll make clear. I met his "Mom" a couple of times and liked her.

By the time I began to love Bill, town gossip said he'd knocked up three local women, maybe more. One took him to court and forced him to marry her. Marriage, though, didn't restrain him much.

I knew he liked me, for at the street dances he began hanging around, joshing: we were funny together, exchanging jokes, digs, and smutty remarks. I knew bunches of male slang. Women up here try to match men in talking filthy. You squelch your male opponent's gab by asserting yours. In our jousts Griffin seldom raised his voice, and never shouted me down.

Why I liked a guy with a soiled reputation I don't know. He never threatened me. And all summer, when I'd run into him he seemed to shine on to me, and I liked it. I felt he had Christmas tree lights around his belly, if you know what I mean; it was hard to cast my eyes elsewhere. While no one would have accused Hurley of hanky-panky (as it turned out, while he was dating me he had an older woman in Chicago whom he married after our break-up), Griffin promised new rules for the mating game. Maybe if Hurley hadn't acted so middle-aged—he was only twenty-five, but because of his slight paunch reminded me of how Dad stood and sat—I'd have acted more like a betrothed female. Despite the crappy ring and the paper announcement, I never believed I'd end up as Mrs. Nell Remington. I never missed Hurley when he was in Chicago.

On the last street dance of the summer (they ended on Labor Day), I'd been chatting with friends and feeling good at being free of Remington. Engagement to him seemed unreal, and, until I knew he was arriving on his bi-monthly visits to see his mom and me (always in that order), I kept his ring under socks and underwear in my dresser.

Since the news of our engagement was in the paper, I assumed Bill Griffin knew of it.

That evening, as I usually did, I danced with girl friends. Shirley Congleton liked waltzes where we'd take turns leading, i.e., being the man. I liked her blonde curls tight against my cheek. With Dolores Birch I danced the "Wipe-Out."

Occasionally Charlie would take a break from playing, climb down from the hay wagon, have a beer, and take a turn along the street while the other musicians kept playing. On one break—it was nearly 9:30 according to the First National Bank clock—he asked me to dance. I started to sweat, but before I could say no we were fox-trotting through the crowd. Despite his leg brace he was agile, never breaking tempo. He held me close. I felt my breasts flatten against his shirt when he pressed his hand against my back, low, where my buttocks began. In breaking from me, he kissed my cheek and said I was a good partner. If he only knew!

I moved to the fringes, for I had to quiet my feelings. Well, girl, I thought, you've had your fling, so get on with the show. I was smart enough to realize I'd never capture Charlie.

As I moved towards Shirley, Bill Griffin stopped in front of me. "Nell," he said. "I thought I'd go check out the Marathon County Fair in Wausau. Want to come along?"

"Sure," I said. "Why not?"

On the way to the car he said: "You don't play women's silly games." He laughed. "Great. I won't push, and once I drop you off later tonight, I'll prowl around on my own. I'll find a woman." He drew a hand across his lips. "None of those gals matter to me; but they do matter to *Throckmorton* down here between my legs. Once he has a spin, he's OK for a few more hours."

Bringing in the Corpse

B ILL DROVE one of the family's two hearses, the smaller one, the Cadillac used mainly for fetching corpses to the mortuary. When old Griffin got word from the sheriff of a death he'd send Bill out to fetch the remains. The larger hearse, in the garage, was a brown Cadillac with silver swan hub-caps, sloping roof and windows, and tasseled shades that could be shut for privacy. The regular driver of the big hearse was Ben Sturges, a local figure who usually wore striped pants, top hat, and white gloves. Both his height of over six feet and his cascading but solid-looking paunch said "Security. You're safe with me." In what better hands could you set out for the after-life? He was so brown—hair, complexion, etc.—that he looked made of caramel. He was old P. J. Griffin's right-hand man.

The hearse driver, of course, sat up front, blocked off from the back area used for stretchers and a folding trolley. Since the law required that an attendant accompany corpses, a small green folding seat dropped down a few inches from the body. In a town as small as Eagle River, no officials other than a rare state inspector would check to see that the law was observed.

I climbed in beside Bill and joked about the skeleton jouncing on a small spring over the rear-view mirror, along with some felt dice. A naked celluloid kewpie doll completed his collection.

The Marathon County Fair was large. By throwing baseballs, Bill won a stuffed doll with sunflower petals around her head, clown cheeks, and scarlet lips. He said it looked like me. A compliment? We started home about 2 a.m. Though Bill had downed several beers, he wasn't drunk.

"Bill," I said as we drove towards Rhinelander, "I'd line your coffin in black with a black satin pillow trimmed in pink. I'd place snapshots of naked women over your groin."

"Be sure to throw in some iced beers," he laughed. "Your coffin would have black polka dots, a lace shroud, and for your pillow a slab of yellow birch drilled full of holes by flickers."

"I hate polka dots."

"I'll put my creation on display in Granddad's slumber room for the whole town to see. I'll set your lips in a smirk. One jaw I'll plug with more cotton than the other. Your *life lumps*."

"Black's the color of your shitty character," I jibed. "And the pink on your pillow stands for all the women you've screwed."

The following Thursday Bill phoned the A&W and asked me to go with him to Sayner. He had to pick up an old farmer who'd died that afternoon. "I'll see you at 3:30," he said.

After leaving St. Germaine, we passed a doe lying where she'd been struck by a car. Huge ravens were shredding strips of meat. "Stop, Bill," I said. I ran over to the deer. "It's sure dead." The birds had already stabbed out its eyeballs, and the rear right leg was gone up to the haunch. A coyote's razor teeth had sliced both flesh and bone.

Bill pointed to a towering alder. On the very top was a bald eagle. While eagles prefer live fish, often stealing them from osprey, they do eat carrion. Once we drove off, he'd swoop down with talons bared, grabbing possession, and stuffing himself at leisure. I'm glad to say these eagles are numerous again; for in the fifties DDT softened their shells and they almost died out. Since the seventies, when the poison was banned, they've been bouncing back.

DDT once was seen as a miracle. Planes sprayed the whole town, killing mosquitoes, which was great for the tourist industry. We were so dumb that when we heard a plane, we'd rush into the back yard and stand under a shower of DDT.

The old man's house sat in a yard full of fire weed and thistles. Morning glory vines covered the rusty composition siding. As we drove up, two tortoise-shell cats sped off. The front door was open. Apparently, whoever found the man had forgotten to shut it. Behind the house was a lake, more of a pond, which must have been shallow, for a low marsh was choking it. An oarless wooden boat lay on its side in the weeds.

"Wait here, Nell. It won't be pretty. I'll call when I've got him on the stretcher."

I imagined the man's grizzled face peeking through the window curtains. Dad always believed that when someone dies alone their spirit remains behind, ready for space-travel. His own dad, he claimed, actually turned up sitting in the old Sundstein house. He sat there not talking, looking so solid that Dad greeted him. That same day, Dad learned that Richard Peters died in Muncie, Indiana.

This may sound silly, but I believe in mysterious energies a-flow. Don't knock 'em. The dead keep touching us. That's why on Memorial Day I stick plastic flowers on Mom's and Dad's graves, a ritual my daughter Marilyn helps me with. I wish you had more regard for the dead, Bob. To say "death is a natural process" robs the dignity and some of the love you had for the dear one departed.

"You can come in now," Bill called.

The house smelled of kerosene, charcoal, mackinaw jackets, and overalls. Scraps of fried fish and potatoes sat on a plate on a formica table drawn up to the window. Off the room serving as both kitchen and living room, past a rusty pot-bellied stove with a scroll-work top, was a small bedroom. The body was there wrapped in sheets. Bill maneuvered it onto a stretcher. "He's all shrivelled up," Bill said.

Corpses have never startled me, and it isn't only because Everett forced me to kiss them. I've always been a realist, or whatever you call it. Of course, I've never seen a real messy accident with guts squashed and mangled. I don't know if I'd be brave or not. I just don't want people staring at me, and that won't happen if my kids obey my wishes. For me, I don't want cremation. Who wants to be a pile of ashes with scraps of bone the fire didn't burn up? I want to rot in peace. Let the worms eat me.

I grabbed one end of the stretcher and Bill took the other.

"He's not as messy as some," Bill said.

We slid the body into the hearse. "I'd like you to ride back there," said Bill. "The law says that someone has to."

"What the hell," I said. The seat dropped down facing the body. I could reach out and touch the old man, who was flat on his back, the sheet now wound tightly around his head giving the effect of a mummy, or of an auto accident victim swirled in bandages. Bill had tied the body down with webbing.

"We're off," Bill shouted back through the sliding glass window separating the cab from my part of the vehicle. Since this hearse was used mainly for retrieving corpses, its interior was plain, with steel ribbing forming the shell. The shell itself still had a rusty primer coat of paint. The noise of churning axles as we hit ruts and potholes was deafening.

We'd driven about ten minutes when the corpse shuddered, gurgling (was it my imagination?) and writhed beneath its straps. When I shouted, Bill stopped the vehicle, jumped out, and came around.

"The sonofabitch is not dead," I shouted. "Look," I pointed.

The old guy had drawn his knees up, loosening the straps, and, with his head still covered, had twisted his neck and was facing where I'd been sitting.

"He won't eat you," Bill laughed. "That's just good old rigor mortis setting in."

"Why didn't you tell me? I'll have a heart attack!" I didn't want this old fart chasing me, his bandages like gauze streaming from a shredded battle flag.

"Come in front," Bill said, taking my arm. "I've seen this happen so often I didn't think about it. I'm sorry."

"I've news for you, boy. You won't do this to me again, ever."

For the rest of the trip, Bill smiled but remained quiet. When we reached my house, he turned to me. The car was chilly, as though the fall air which socks this area in September and then lifts for a few days during a glorious Indian summer of colored maple leaves, and then returns for winter, had arrived.

"Nellie," he said. "There's some trouble. I can't see you for awhile. I'm sorry."

He wouldn't explain.

"I'm sorry," I said. "We've had a great time."

Losing Bill to a surprise marriage chimed with my spurning Hurley. The freedom I enjoyed with Bill showed me how boring life was with Hurley. I did not love him and never could. Even if romantic novels were half true, nothing stirred me towards Hurley. Also, I saw a post office brochure inviting people to sign on in the Women's Army Corps. High school, where I was a lousy student (I'd be a senior), was, as they say, a wash. I was prepared for nothing but grinding, ordinary work.

The WACs appealed to me. Bob, you were drafted into the Army in 1943 and Everett enlisted much later, to escape mortgages he'd gotten on land Dad had given him. You survived your three-year duty, even saving up, as I said, to buy our house in town. You were at the university in Madison, on the GI Bill, working towards your Ph.D. Who guessed you'd end up as a poet and professor? According to the WACs recruiting officer, I would be trained as I chose, preferably in mechanics, continuing the trade Dad had already taught me.

The dregs of Indian summer: the area still flowed with the reds, oranges, and yellows of sugar maples. If you were on a lake, and the shores were lined with blazing trees, and the sun was still up, you traversed a liquid carpet of amazing color. I've never seen anything like those perfect late falls for ending old affairs and starting new ones. The break with Hurley was smooth.

He'd phoned to say he was so busy in Chicago he'd be home only once the whole month. He was an unskilled assembly line worker making cam shafts. Also, he wanted to see the last of the fall color.

"I'll be here," I said.

Losing Bill, instead of sending me back to Hurley's arms, increased my dislike for the guy. I'd rather go it alone, and, anyway, the WACs had accepted me. I'd go as soon as I graduated.

When Hurley appeared, before he entered the house, I said: "We have to talk."

He pushed right past me as though he hadn't heard. He wore a new Stetson, faun with a wide brim, pulled gangster-fashion over his eyes. I shivered with contempt. "Take off that silly hat," I said.

"I thought you'd like it." He turned the brim in his hands.

"Give me the damn thing," I said, grabbing it, putting it down on a table near Mom's pink geraniums. "You look like the dumbest member of Al Capone's gang."

He set about greeting my family and settled into a ratty over-stuffed chair near some African violets and the Christmas cactus which was putting forth red blossoms. General chatter about his job. Some local news: more deer killed on highways than ever, a new cemetery vault for holding bodies until the ground thawed in spring, the death of a Morgan twin, the twins being the owners of the oldest grocery in town and descendants of the first white male born in the county.

I sat there on the horse-hair couch waiting, twisting the engagement ring round my finger. I feared I'd never get it off. I had flashes of Bill. Was he in bed with his wife? Was he out raising hell, missing me?

When my parents went to bed around nine, their usual time, Hurley joined me on the sagging couch.

"I can't marry you, Hurley," I said.

He wasn't upset. "Is it Griffin?" he asked.

"I'm joining the WACs. I have to do more with my life."

"You're no dyke, are you?"

"You're really stupid," I snapped. "You're why I won't marry you." I thrust my hand with the ring on it towards him. "Here, take the damn thing back. I don't want it."

He pried the ring off, gave a wimpy sigh, and dropped it in his pocket.

"Some good woman will be glad to wear this," he said, getting up from the couch.

"Well, it's making the rounds," I said. "Didn't Victoria Dolansky return it?"

"So what?" he managed a self-satisfied grin. Then, yawning, he announced he was going to the Deerskin to see his folks.

That was the last I saw of him. The next month he married that Chicago woman. Any idiot could tell he'd been seeing her all the time he was making trips up here to see me.

6

Nights with the Undertaker's Grandson

THE SCHOOL YEAR passed. Teachers let up on graduating seniors, concluding we'd already learned whatever we'd take from school. I took advantage of that, working twenty hours a week frying hamburgers at the A&W. Minimum wage, yes, but I needed cash for expenses during basic training, before my first government check. I looked forward to the Army, and clipped pictures of WACs from newspapers and magazines. I fantasized a natty uniform and giving smart salutes. I loved the notion of a sisterhood defending the country. And the Korean War was in full swing.

The time for induction approached. I was to take a train from Minocqua to Milwaukee, register at a hotel reserved for inductees, take physical and mental tests, and then go to a basic training camp.

My main unfinished business, I felt, was sexual. Here I was, an eighteen-year-old virgin full of images of the bliss sex was supposed to give, once you'd hooked the right guy. It was a female's birthright. So far I'd missed out. Sex before going into the Army might mature me, I naively thought.

The day before Dad was to drive me to Minocqua, to the train, I packed. I wasn't to take much, a change of clothes, tooth brush, and whatever sundries I wanted.

I remember sitting with Mom. It was about 3 o'clock, and I'd just come back from saying goodbys at the A&W. My bags were ready to go. I'd even bought a romance novel at the Rexall Store. I was nervous, and so was Mom. Dad was in his shop welding. Violets on the living room wallpaper suddenly crowded in on me. The Christmas cactus waved little red tongues. I started pacing the room.

"It won't be long now, baby." Mom paused. "If you want to help, we

104

can start supper." We were having my favorite meal, Swiss steak braised in onion gravy, with mashed potatoes.

"I'm too jumpy," I said. "I'll be back in an hour."

I walked to Main street and circled the Information Booth three or four times before dropping a dime in the pay phone. *Ring. Ring. Ring.* "Bill?"

"Yes," came the voice. I'd heard he was separated from his wife, and had a room above Love's Tavern.

"Bill, pick me up tonight, as soon as it's dark. I go to the WACs tomorrow, and I want to spend some of tonight with you."

"Sure. I'll be there about seven. We can take a ride out by the Wisconsin River, near the Flowage." He knew what I wanted.

The flowage is a place where the Wisconsin River rampages before pounding along downstate eventually flowing into the Mississippi. Under a three-quarter moon, the river fills with jewels, agate and silver-toned. Because of the pure air and the elevation of nearly fifteen hundred feet, the stars seem so near you can grab them. A narrow road leaves Highway 70 and leads to the river shore where a pair of picnic benches are set up for enjoying the scenery.

When he approached the river, Bill turned off the head lights. I moved through a dream. A horned owl flew past, briefly blocking the moon.

Bill moved close. "You wanted to see me?"

"Yes. I don't think the Army should get a virgin, do you?"

"Well, I'm not surprised."

"I can't think of anyone I'd rather do it with than you, sweetheart."

I moved over to Bill in the driver's seat (he'd borrowed his Grand-dad's big Cadillac) and stroked the back of his neck, tracing my fingers through his hair. Sure, I was nervous. The glossy river just lay there between the trees. The trees themselves moved, ruffled by one of those breezes that predict a storm. Bill's right hand on my thigh felt like mouse whiskers; then, he pushed deeper. I had stupidly brought my leg up so that I was half-sitting on it, you know—in some weird yoga position, forcing him to dig harder than he might otherwise have had to. A trickle of sweat dropped from my chin. I pulled his hand back. "Wait," I said. He withdrew his hand.

"What the hell," I thought. "You wanted this to happen, girl. So, get on with it. Stop being a ninny." The musty interior of the sedan smelled like crushed walnuts blent with the stink of gasoline.

I fumbled unbuttoning Bill's shirt. He loosened my bra. "Let's climb in back," he said.

Getting out of my jeans was a struggle, but I managed to kick them past my heels and plop into the back seat. Bill's body looked milky in the moonlight. He pressed my hand on his organ, against the head.

I stretched out on the vinyl, which felt clammy and cold. Bill eased on top of me. A celluloid kewpie doll in a hula skirt, hung over the rear-view mirror, was jiggling. When Bill rammed, I feared I'd douse us with blood. "Be careful," I said. "Go slow."

"Sure, sure," he said softly, quavering.

Then he really shoved. There was smarting, a friction like sand-paper, and I realized there was nothing I could do. More desperate than loving, I clung to his thumping body. None of the skyrockets I'd expected exploded. Bill had his twenty-second climax, shuddering, whimpering, shooting, sighing, and withdrawing, afterwards wiping his penis on my panties. I felt used. I might just as well have been a knothole in a board. I had not bled.

We got dressed, he standing on the driver's side of the car, and I on the other. "Well, how was it, Nell?"

"Okay," I murmured across the top of the car. Dew had settled on the metal.

We drove in silence back to town, where he dropped me at my folks. "Be in touch," he said, with a quick kiss. His car tail lights were obscene winks. I entered the house to sleep in my bed for the last time for months. If my imagination had been more active, I might have pictured spermy squiggles possessing my female crannies, seeking out ovaries to pierce. But I didn't. I thought they'd pass into the toilet with my pee.

The Company of Women

CAPTAIN Oriole B. Stout, Commander, Company I, Second Battalion, Women's Army Corps, Training Center, Fort Lee, Virginia, greeted forty-eight raw recruits standing at ragged attention in the mess hall. If we expected a sweet mother figure we were wrong. Flanking her were two first lieutenants, in sharp uniforms, looking mean in their neat short curls, ready to pounce. I'd been in camp for only three hours when, with forty-seven other women, I was shepherded by two sergeants and two corporals to this "welcome."

This is my recollection of Captain Stout's remarks: "You are now part of the United States Army. We shall transform you from civilians to soldiers. Things may be rough, depending on whether or not you've got the guts. Now, at this precise moment in time you are not civilians, nor are you soldiers. You are lower than bugs crawling on their bellies in the dirt. You are nothing. From here on in you will say 'Yes Ma'am' and 'No Ma'am.' We will tell you when to sleep, get up, eat, work, and what to wear. Now, I will turn you over to your sergeants and corporals. I hope that if I ever see any of you in my office that it will be a positive experience. I do not allow any foul-ups in this company."

She was awesome as she did a right face, and, without looking back, with a shake of her bobbed hair, disappeared out the door through which she'd come.

The sergeants appeared, told us to sit at the mess tables, and hinted that they might be people. Ever since I climbed on board the train for Milwaukee, arriving there, going through a physical exam and a mental test, and being thrown a dress with tan stripes, I hoped I'd manage my Army life with the support, of course, of peers, sergeants, and officers. These were my naive thoughts as I rode through Virginia in the dark, peering up at the stars, talking with another recruit, Mary Proctor, from Milwaukee, who was just as dumb as me about the future. With such beautiful sky views, the world had to make sense.

Sergeant Butterfield, a beefy woman with bright red hair and a Southern accent, outranked the sergeant in charge of the second platoon. "Privates. We are going to close this first day with a party. After you have downed your mashed potatoes, pork chops, and cherry cobbler, you are all to meet here and then we'll march to the supply house and get stuff for our party.".

Eating, we soon found, was as much supervised as any activity, including the latrine, which was set up with a row of "thunder mugs," all without partitions. Once in line for chow, we picked up trays, which we thrust towards the servers. The food was slammed onto the trays. "Flop, splash, thunk." Waiting by the garbage cans where we dumped our left-over food were the sergeants. If we'd wasted food, they ordered us back to eat all that ended up on our plates. Even so, plenty was left over, and much was not even served to begin with. The company next to us, with twice as many women, got the same amount as our company. All left-over food was hauled off by a local farmer for his pigs.

In our "party," each of us was handed a mop, pail, and scrub brush and were ordered back to the barracks. The floor around our canvas cot was to be "so you could eat off it." The steel closet at the head of our bed, where we hung our uniforms, and the wooden footlocker where we stored sundries and personal items were to shine.

I was more naive than most recruits, or so it seemed to me. The easy cheer I'd managed during high school was of no use now. I sure was jolted. When I tried to charm the Company Commander, I assumed that the Army was like the democracy I'd known, and that everyone, all friendly, would pull together.

Towards the end of my second week, during guard duty, Captain Stout, at midnight, strode officiously up to me and, in a voice she'd use reading from a military manual, demanded: "Private, is the base secured?" I felt like laughing, saluted, and said that everything was safe. I felt silly with the whistle around my neck and the flashlight in my hand—which women carried on guard in lieu of the rifles men carried. Consider the sexism: females were considered incapable of defending the nation even if the Korean War got worse. In those days, feminism had not reared its head (if you'll pardon the sexist expression), so there was no possibility of our taking up battle stations.

When I caught a smile on Captain Oriole B. Stout's face, I decided to warm her up more: "Do you come from a small town, too?" I asked.

"Private," she snapped, "return to your post." The message was clear: the barrier between the Commander and us women, though invisible, was as solid as a ten-foot brick wall.

My effort to reach Sergeant Butterfield misfired even worse. When I joshed with her about separating men's and women's units on base, and asked how she felt, she sneeringly replied: "Speak only when you're spoken to."

What helped me through these nightmarish weeks were the other recruits. My cot stood near the outside wall of the platoon sergeant's room. Next to me was Adelaide Proctor, an Illinois farm girl, who also hoped for motor-pool duties. She was short, with mousey brown hair, and as burly as I was. We looked after one another, checking to see that our beds were OK, and that our uniforms were proper. Not only were we the first recruits spied by the Sergeant on leaving her room, but our last names began with the same letter: "Peters and Proctor." "Peters and Proctor." Like despised Siamese twins we were always picked for shift details. Sick of this, I faced the Sergeant: "Are Peters and Proctor the only recruits here? Why can't you see beyond our two cots when you need slave 'volunteers'?"

"So you think I'm unfair?"

"Yes," I said, falling into her trap.

"Well, Private, you don't know what *unfair* is." She paused. "Peters and Proctor," she ordered, "Report to the Officers' Quarters and paint the shower rooms, all pipes, walls, nooks, and crannies. You have three hours for the job. Stop by the Supply Room and pick up a gallon of battleship gray and brushes and get to work."

"Why punish Proctor?" I asked.

"Shut up!" she ordered. "Do as you're told."

Three hours later, Butterfield appeared with the C.O., examined our paint job, which we were just finishing, praised it, and turned to the C.O., who told her she'd wanted aluminum, not battleship gray. We couldn't believe it! We got the new paint and did not finish until after 9 P.M. We'd missed evening chow, and were worn out.

I'd assumed that since this was a world of females, there would be a sisterhood. At home, I never felt inferior to anyone, and saw most people as equal. Sure, there were always a few asshole ego maniacs, as in every society; but in Eagle River I probably enjoyed as close to live-and-let-live as was possible anywhere. Here, at Ft. Lee, the rigid order made robots of recruits. Yet, I vowed that the officers would never kill my spirit, although they succeeded in the sense that I had to conceal my true feelings. I hoped, as other girls did, that once we finished Basic Training we'd regain dignity and ourselves become NCOs and even officers. If I ever got that high, I'd be friendly and caring.

An experience occurred late one October evening which merely deepened my disillusion. As barracks policewoman, my duty was to make rounds during the night. I was taking a break near some top steps when I heard crying. I found Charley Youngman huddled in her bed. She was slender, with short auburn hair, small fine-boned face with sweetheart lips, and long fingers. "What's wrong, Charley?" I asked.

"I, I can't take this, Nellie. I'm missing my kids, two of them, so bad. My husband took them when we got divorced. I miss my little girl the worst. She died of diphtheria a month ago." Charley still wore her wedding ring, single with a tiny diamond, but she wore it on her right hand.

I patted her shoulder. "It's hard, Charley. Things will look better in the morning."

"Hug me, Nellie," she said.

The next day the Captain summoned me to her office. "We've had reports," she said, "that you were with Pvt. Youngman last night while you were on duty. Is that true?"

I explained that Youngman was very distressed and that I had done what I could to comfort her. "Yesterday was her birthday, and one of her baby daughters died last month."

"I want to know specifically how you comforted her?" she snapped. "With words or intimate gestures?"

"Words, Sir. Words."

"We've been watching you two. We've had trouble with Youngman before, and I have my eye on her." She paused for a couple of minutes or more. "Do you know what happens to lesbians?"

"To what?"

"Come on, girl. You're not that stupid. You know what I mean."

"Some women like women more than men. But I've not heard that word before."

"You *are* straight off the farm. In the WACs," she shouted, "lesbians are dishonorably discharged. So watch your p's and q's. I'm separating you two for your own good, Peters. You'll thank me some day." She transferred me to a new platoon, leaving Charley where she was, for easy monitoring.

Charley helped me push my duffel bag to the flag pole where the buses stopped. Just before I climbed aboard she threw her arms around me, gave me a kiss, and thanked me. She hoped we'd stay in touch.

I hung in for nearly six weeks. Though my normal menstrual

period was delayed, I didn't worry, for I understood that the physical and mental stress of my new life could delay the cycle. By the ninth week I'd lost my appetite, felt drained, and knew something was wrong.

When I signed for Sick Call, the captain called me in. "Private Peters," she said, "I see you're signed up on sick call. What's wrong?"

I described my symptoms and said I'd missed two periods. "I can't go near the mess hall without feeling sick, and I can't eat once I get there."

She rifled through some papers as though she'd forgotten me. Obviously, she was stalling.

"Is that all, Captain?" I asked.

She looked up with her hands extended along both sides of her pile of papers, much as a man would, and said that I needed to get my mind off my problems. "The Sergeant will assign you to another work detail loading supplies at the warehouse. And another thing, if you don't eat right you won't get anywhere with me."

When I said I had to see a doctor, she dismissed me; there was no more to discuss.

That evening she positioned herself in such a way as to be sure I had food on my tray. All I took was a small carton of milk and some jello.

"Peters," she called. "That's not enough. Go back through the line and get more food."

The entree that night was what we called "shit on a shingle," a mix of ground beef with onions in a pallid gravy thrown over a hunk of toast, the whole mixture looking like dog puke. I took the food, lingered at the table, then managed to sneak past her and dump the stuff in the garbage. Oh, how I ached to be in Eagle River. I started shaking and weeping. I had to go home. I didn't know how I would do it, but I had to go home.

Pink or Blue?

IN ANOTHER two weeks Basic Training would end, we would graduate and, after a month's furlough, would be sent to other bases for specialized training and our Army duties as professionals. I still hoped for the motor pool, but the powers that be decided on clerk typist—just why, I never figured out.

My fatigue and nausea persisted. My diet was mainly of milk, juice, coffee, toast, some fruit, and jello. I never again signed on for sick call, for to do so I risked chores imposed by the Captain for gold bricking. I felt that if I could hang on until my furlough, away from Army life, once more at home, I'd recover my health and sanity. I ached for the pines and lakes and the deer leaping over the roads. My problems, I realized, were psychological; my hatred for the Army was very deep. Missing home became part of the quilt-work of my life.

Army graduation was simple. Our battalion was honored for completing basic training in record time. We marched in formation to Headquarters, where the commanding colonel stood and where Captain Stout issued certificates. Among his brief congratulations, the colonel predicted that some of us would see Korea, backing up American troops who were now in the thick of the war.

Back at the barracks we waited for rosters announcing our new assignments. Most, including me, were destined for Ft. Dix, New Jersey. The next day, on furlough, I entrained for Chicago, and continued via a spur route to Monico, twenty-five miles from Eagle River, where I hitched a ride home. After a month I would report to Dix.

Although Mom and Dad were living in a new two-bedroom cinder-block house near Dad's welding and blacksmith shop on Highway 70, little had changed: the same battery of plants Mom had in the earlier house were here, the same rickety horse-hair furniture and the junk cherry-wood rockers, ugly throwbacks to earlier days and big farm houses. Mom crocheted brightly-colored afghans to cover the furniture. Dad now had a small black-and-white television which sat opposite his rocker; he watched mostly boxing and wrestling (he called it "wrassling") matches. Although Mom had cooked a chicken dinner, I couldn't eat. While my folks now had separate bedrooms, as long as I was home, they moved their beds together. Mom complained of Dad's snores, which shook the house.

Dad was first to be suspicious: "You're not too well, are you, Kiddo?"

I told him that the WACs was rough, and I was lucky I'd survived. The next round would be easier. I was still hoping to be a mechanic, though the roster at Dix said "clerk-typist."

He insisted I see Doc Barney. Mom was concerned when I reported that I'd missed three periods. "For any girl your age, something's wrong."

Doc Barney was shocked to find my blood count a little over six. It should have been fourteen. "What are they doing to you?" he asked. "You'll be dead with this blood count."

He checked more, using the standard test: if your blood when mixed with frog urine tested pink, you were pregnant. Mine was *very* pink.

That afternoon I told Mom I was going to take a long walk to the old Sundstein place, near Mud Minnow Lake, to do some thinking.

"You know the house is gone," Mom said. "The new owners have put up a modern one. They'd let you go back on the land, if you asked."

Once I left Highway 70, a half mile from my folks' new house, I turned left onto Sundstein, and shortly reached swirling, roiling Mud Creek where it spilled through a large galvanized culvert under the road. Here I inhaled lungfulls of balsam and pine. Though it was late October, a few sugar maples still held colored leaves, mere rags of their earlier glory. Where the sun splashed along the trunks of white birch, the trees seemed to glow.

I moved quietly to avoid scaring any animals. A gray fox scampered across the road, carrying a limp rabbit. A woodpecker jabbed his beak into wood, harsh and loud, although I could not locate him. A red-tailed hawk dove in a perfect figure eight before plummeting behind the pines. Nearby, a partridge drummed his wings as he rose towards the marsh; these birds often had difficulty getting airborne—their meaty breasts seemed out of proportion to their wings. Perhaps they should have cross-bred with loons—those tread water surfaces before going aloft. A loon's legs and feet are far back on his body, for gaining speed. If you've ever seen a loon on land, which they avoid, you'll know that they half-wiggle forwards on their bodies as though part snake. No bird call is as sad. I was probably lucky not to hear one that afternoon—for the loon has always been my special bird. Though they pair for life, it takes a large lake to support two such couples— they are very territorial. And it's rare that you see them, although, especially on autumn evenings and at dawn, you hear their music. I'm sure that suicides are inspired by loon songs.

I passed a marsh of blueberry bushes, lantern flowers, and black spruce. These spruce, numerous here, let you see how marsh lands change into highlands. All over northern Wisconsin you see evidence

of former lakes now entirely choked with trees and shrubs. When gla-
ciers dumped their boulders, they gouged "kettles," as they're called,
and these filled with water, producing the lakes. Experts say that none
of these lakes is over forty feet deep.

I walked onto a moss-covered bog. Reaching down, I pushed my
fingers under to the dank, damp wood rot fertilizing the bog. How cold
it was! And how tender were the tiny rose-shaped and lily-cupped moss
blossoms glowing on top. I grabbed up moss and pressed it to my cheek,
almost as though this plant and this earth mothered me. I squeezed the
moss, crying, then dropped the plants near the black earthy scar I had
made by removing them. I plucked cranberry flowers, some princess
pine, and a few alder leaves and crushed them into a pulp. Opening my
jeans, I smeared the pulp all across my belly where the child was
growing. A sign from the earth. I would keep my child.

Eagle River seemed almost glamorous. Yes, the hodgepodge of
buildings, some with corrugated tin fronts, rust-colored, dating from
the twenties, none more than two stories tall, built of narrow clap-
boards, hadn't changed. Other buildings were in plain styles, like
squares of stucco and sand with glass fronts. There were the cases at
the sporting goods stores where trophy-worthy musky, bass, and walleyes were displayed, all labelled with weight, length, lake of origin,
and name and address of the fisherman. A candy store specialized in a
dozen kinds of fudge. There were copper kettles in the windows where
you watched the candy being made. There was also a cheese cake
bakery with many varieties, their most popular being something called
"the turtle," a dog's supper of nuts, cheese, chocolate, and flavorings.
Since cheese cake was too exotic for the locals, the buyers were almost
always tourists from Milwaukee and Chicago. The old ice cream parlor, Zimpleman's, was gone, although Francis Johnson's camera shop
was there, as was Mulrooney's drug store with its hump-backed owner
busy behind the counter. Two stores lured tourists with gewgaws,
plastic Indians, humorous fishing plaques of varnished birch and pine,
birch bark canoes and tepees, and a few authentic wood carvings of
deer, game birds, and fish. You could buy mounted deer heads and any
game fish you wanted to take back to the city and pretend you'd
snagged them. Yes, and don't forget the bars, from the oldest of all,
The Mint on Wall Street, to the Northwoods (Dad's favorite), and
Bandow's on Main. The old Chicago Northwestern Depot was boarded

up. Train service ended over ten years before, and tourists who once took the "Fisherman's Special" now flew in biplanes up to Land O'Lakes. Above the Vilas Theater, Doc Barney still had his offices. Here I got liver extract shots, and slowly my iron count rose, restoring my energy.

It's hard now to recall how I spent all those furlough days. I guess I was numbed by the pregnancy, and although I was nineteen, my mental age was more like fifteen. Perhaps our folks, by being so permissive, delayed our growing up. During my seventh-month check, Doc Barney took X-rays which he pinned up over a glass with a light behind them. "See this?" he said. The image looked blurred, like a double exposure. It was a double exposure! I would have twins! The sexes? Doc couldn't say.

I was floored, as were Mom and Dad.

When I told Dad that Bill Griffin was the pa, he threatened: "We'll twist his nuts in a wringer." Yet, it took him days to get up the nerve to face Bill's Granddad, the undertaker P. J. Griffin, to ask for Bill's whereabouts.

On Twisting His Nuts in a Wringer

—⟨⟩⟨⟩⟨⟩—

"HE'S OFF somewhere," said P. J. "Got divorced, I hear. Don't know where he is. If he turns up I'll let you know."

Dad was always intimidated by powerful people, the judge, the district attorney, the mayor. Yet, he'd always boast that he got on with them, that everybody liked him, and then he'd stand before them like a child. He reminded me of a character in Dickens—Copperfield, wasn't it, asking for more porridge. I didn't blame Dad then, and I don't blame him now. Considering the strikes he had against him: the death of his mother when he was only four, abandoned by his dad to live by himself on the prairie at age seven, attending school only through second grade. Yet, he could have sent the sheriff after Griffin. If the County Welfare had to support me and my kids, they'd have found him. Only later, after I'd returned to Dix, did Dad wangle Bill's address from his grandfather.

How did I feel about Bill? Well, that we had sex that night was my doing—so he wasn't at fault. And, yes, we were careless. He hadn't used a condom. What hurt most was his answer once the births happened. But that's getting ahead of the story.

I felt then that no matter how hard I tried to make something of my life I'd be slapped down. Joining the WACs was a declaration of independence. Now that was screwed, too. Also, there was the stigma of being an unmarried mother. Numerous jokes were made about local girls who had sons by different fathers. Back then, if you had a reputation for "putting out," forget it, girl! The County Judge would never be on your side. It's the same old shit: "Women love it, so do it. Just don't plant a flag on the spot once you've rammed 'em. Women love bein' fucked and raped." Christ, I could tell that Judge a thing or two: look what happened to me, all for twenty disgusting seconds of penis push where all the shivering was on his side, and none on mine. As I said, echoing Peggy Lee's song: "Is That All There Is?" I've been singing that one all my life and will probably be singing it when they screw the coffin lid down.

Once I was fully aware of my plight, I stopped my walks to town, except to the doctor's. Whenever I left the house I took side streets. What a contrast! Before I knew I was pregnant, I spiffed up in my uniform and Mom showed me off to women in the beauty parlor.

I was soon anxious to get back to Dix, to see if the Army could/ would do anything. That my life might be ruined scared me. And I had to return to the Fort. If I was discharged, I wanted it to be honorable. If I didn't return, I'd be a deserter. Strange that I showed little uterine swelling. Even up to the end, I could wear most of my clothes.

I shortly wrote to Bill who was living in Macon, Georgia, working for a construction company:

December 23, 1951

Dear Bill,

Through Ben Sturges, Dad got your address. I hear you're doing good in construction. You've got the muscles. I've missed you and am taking this opportunity to let you in on the news. I don't know what you're expecting for Christmas, but I AM expecting! Doc Barney says it's twins. I know that it was my idea that we do things on the night before I left for the WACs, but I never thought they would backfire.

I am asking, Bill, that you do the right thing. Let's get married, and I don't care for how long. I want these babies to have a dad's name.

The Army was rough all through basic training. I am now at home on furlough before returning to Ft. Dix. I'm in a mess, and don't know quite what to do. My folks say I (and you) should keep the kids. What do you say?

I return to Dix next week and will see the Commanding Officer about my future. I feel all up in the air.

With love,

Nell, the mother of your kids

On returning to Dix, once I had settled into my new barracks and had unpacked my clothes, I sought permission to see the C.O., to whom I presented my transfer papers and explained I was pregnant. She was unhappy to hear that my Fort Lee C.O. had pooh-poohed my symptoms and wouldn't let me see a doctor. Only on furlough, I explained, did I learn the truth.

"Does the baby's father know?" She seemed considerate. Though she was only in her late thirties, she had graying hair, and her eyes were friendly.

"Yes," I answered. "We finally located him. I've written, but so far he's not answered."

"What do you think you should do, Private?"

"M'am. I don't know. It's hopeless."

"Perhaps I can help. First, don't feel you've betrayed the Army. These things have happened often. Of six women I counselled recently, five have put their babies up for adoption and are continuing their Army careers. It's an important decision, obviously. Who comes first, the mother or the baby? Only you can answer that."

I thanked her, saluted, and turned to leave.

"Let me know what the father says. We'll work from there. In the meantime, you'll be excused from duties until after the birth. You can catch up later on your clerk-typist training."

37 Link Street
Macon, Georgia

December 30, 1952

Nell:

I'm not the father. The Army would not have admitted you if you were pregnant, and the tests would have shown you were. You've been playing around up there, right? So, don't try to trap me. Bug off! I've been in this situation before, and am pretty capable of getting out of it. I don't want to hurt you, but you'd better go after the right guy. Being in touch with me will get you nowhere. My Grandfather has a lot of pull with the Judge, as I'm sure your Dad knows.—BILL

Women's Army Corps
Ft. Dix, New Jersey

January 2, 1952

Bill,
    Your reply is upsetting and mean. The Commanding Officer said I should go after you, and that they would use their services to help me. Other WACs have been in my shoes (although I don't know of any with twins) and have survived. I'd hoped you would come through. I said you were decent.
    I've come round to my folks' way of thinking and will have the babies in Eagle River. I'll get my Honorable Discharge.
    I so hope you'll be standing there beside my hospital bed looking down at us.—Nell

    I reported the chilling news to the C.O. and asked for the discharge. Within three weeks I was at home sorting bits. It might have helped if I'd had all the pieces, but I didn't, and could only guess where the missing ones were, or what sort of picture they'd finally add up to.

The Music Goes Round and Round

I WAS HUSKY for a woman, with wide shoulders and big arms. Although my weight before pregnancy, at the time of my enlistment, was 185 pounds, the Induction Center MD recorded my weight at 145, the maximum allowed at the time. He expressed amazement that with this weight I seemed to have so little fat. If I were taller (I'm 5'6") I'd be an Amazon. "Give me the magic spear, High Priestess, and I'll lead your female warriors to battle those horrid men!"
    Perhaps my build explained why my pregnancy showed so little. Until the ninth month I hid the bulge under jackets. I won't lie and tell you that there was no bulge. There was, but you'd have had to look close, and in those weeks nobody was looking at me unless they

were gossips who wanted to stare at something bigger than Mt. Rushmore: an unmarried virgin socked with twins! I could rip their tongues out! That's why I stayed home so much, not wanting to have any eyes wandering like fire over my defenses.

I'd been home a few hours when we were hit by one of those downdraft storms, when hot air wheeling into the upper sky draws cold air after it. Ominous. I went to lock the front door and saw leaping bronze toads. They'd fall down into the packed dirt beside the step, then jump back up. They started huddling, a sure sign of hail; they didn't want to get conked.

These down-drafts aren't true tornadoes. Tornadoes whirl around a vortex and sweep up trees, cars, shacks, chickens, squirrels, and people, and set them down, often without smashing them. The down-drafts are more dangerous since they hop, skip, and jump. No region of the country has worse storms. Also, you will see that trees whirled by tornadoes drop twisted every which way; trees felled by a down-draft always point in the same direction.

Once Dad checked the house for safety, we sat watching through the picture window for the storm to hit. Some clouds were tinged with magenta and a deep rose (for the sun had started going down). Other clouds, indigo, swirled with cottony mist. Lightning etched the sky. Enormous thunder claps. The usual images of gods up there bowling (that's the German fairy tale, right?) seemed vapid for what was really going on. Birch trees, balsam, and spruce whipped about. One spruce snapped off ten feet from the ground and smashed onto our lawn. A motorist, stranded, waited with his engine running, his lights on, his windshield wipers crunching. The man inside was wearing one of those tractor caps with visor.

Then the hail, icy globs of it, drummed on our tarpaper roof. Piles of the stuff formed in the yard. The air was so black we wanted to turn on lights, but Dad said, "No. Let's keep the switches off." A calm followed, and when you thought the worst was over, another deluge slammed in. "Welcome home, Sis," Dad said. "We've pulled out everything including fireworks. Next, it'll be the kitchen sink."

After the storm, we drove to inspect the damage. The Sundstein District was hard hit, although no houses were down. For a couple of miles the storm followed the road, felling trees. Near the culvert area where Mud Creek flowed, downed trees were so thick it seemed that insane beavers had been at work. The creek flowed over the road, its bed diverted a good ten rods from where it had originally been.

I didn't see the storm then as symbolic of my life, and I still don't. Call this reporting the truth, if you want. The storm did occur.

When they were five months old, my fetuses started pushing and jumping. Until then, apart from gas bouts, I was pretty normal; the liver shots helped. My rib cage took the brunt of the kicks. I could see those two guys (I don't know why I assumed they were male) like a pair of dried-up gnomes, without tasselled caps, lying side by side facing one another, jamming their clubby feet into me. "Quit it, you little bastards," I'd say. At times my lungs shook. The infants were so merged, they must have been holding hands, their scrawny rib cages quivering with glee. Of course, since their vision cones were undeveloped, they had to do all of this in the dark. A down-draft effect? Sure.

I wrote away for a *names book*, and decided that if one child was a boy I'd name him Michael David, and if the other was female she'd be Michelle Liegh. For a second boy I'd simply reverse the names to "David Michael," which would be an iron bond between them. Twins without a pa, to put it mildly, would have it rough. Having a mother who wasn't too feminine might help.

Don't get me wrong. I was seldom depressed, and was even euphoric. I would linger for hours by Mud Minnow Lake, sitting under the jack pines, re-familiarizing myself with the lush marsh and water growths: the plants right along the edges—reeds topped with scarlet leaves and berries, and, further out, an array of cattail, wild rice, bulrush, pickerel weed, and arrowhead. When the sun was right you could see the tops of underwater plants—naiads, and sweeps of bullhead lily. And then the birds: orange orioles flocked to the sugar maples; territorial red-winged blackbirds warbled over their harems of nesting females; purple martins, swifts, and bank swallows swooped meals of insects from the air; and there, always, were the screaming jays. As I hunkered on a carpet of bronzed jack-pine needles, I was restored; nourishment soaked my marrow.

I feared my pregnancy would reduce the physical energies of which I was so proud; for they set me above other women, at least among those I knew. To test my force I borrowed an aluminum canoe belonging to Everett and had Dad drive me to the Flowage, a turbulent, boulder-strewn portion of the Wisconsin River, just below the Light and Power plant. The trip would take three hours. Dad said he'd be waiting at the St. Germaine bridge, a logical place to stop; for, once there, if you wished to continue, you'd have to portage the canoe.

Fortunately, I'd brought mosquito lotion, for the insects were big and nasty, as they always are in humid, rainy springs. Jokers call the mosquito the Wisconsin State Bird. Also, because of my freckled skin, I sunburn, so I wore a long-sleeved denim shirt and a brimmed hat.

We launched the canoe below the dam, at a grassy spot hidden from the road by white birch and balsam. Though I had canoed only once before, I felt good, and, seated in the rear with the prow out of the water, began paddling, shooting easily through the first boulders. I waved to Dad. I knew that the current would eventually slacken, and, barring bad winds, the going would get easier. I'd have plenty of time to think.

Around a fast bend I found myself in an area through which there seemed no safe way. The river, over three hundred yards across, was strewn with pools where the flowage swirled around and over each rock, most of them hidden. I thrust forward, crunched the canoe against a rock, rode up, and hung there. While the water was not exactly frigid, it was cold. To right a floundered canoe, to keep my powder dry, and negotiate a hundred yards of river full of sunken logs and turtles, and with musky and northerns with teeth that could shred your hands, scared me.

For ten minutes I paddled, trying for leverage. I was ready to give up, thinking that the only option was to move towards the prow and risk dumping the canoe. I gave one more try, throwing my strength into forward paddle motions while jerking my body. I was free! I left a lot of paint behind on that rock.

Another rapids was smaller than the first, and I soon reached smooth water. Now, however, there were thunder clouds, and jags of lightning flashed to the north, towards Conover. The first spatterings were refreshing, for I had worked up a sweat. I threw back my head, opening my mouth, loving the taste of the fresh rain. I could float now for yards without needing to paddle.

There are moments when you look inside yourself, I find, and then there are these moments when you step outside yourself. You tie few of these to personal problems. That's when you most sing along with nature. I flashed on little scrunched fetus heads lying cheek to cheek, their webbed hands moving softly through the amniotic fluid: I felt the weight of my body in the canoe, and twinges where my thigh bone joins my hip. I wasn't then the chain smoker I am now, so had expansive lungs which sweetened in the pure air. I didn't, though, expect a heron to drop a fish with a Christian symbol in blessing.

As I moved on, I followed a surface chock full of perfectly reflected trees. The watery darkness didn't scare me, that mucky bottom of age-old humus. I skimmed over watery macadam. Like life, right? You don't know what's around the bend, and you can't know how solid (or shaky) the ground (or water) is.

Nests along the route flashed. I'd spot them right off. Wood duck mothers sat on nests people had built and hung from trees. A pair of ducks preferred their own carpentry, throwing up an old-fashioned nest in the top of an oak. Below, ospreys were defending a pile of twigs on top of another man-created nesting platform. You had to use a climbing belt, like those telephone line-men use, or you nailed slats at intervals to reach the thirty-foot height. Nearby in a lofty spruce twisted into lyre-shapes by porcupines feasting on bark, killing the normal upthrust of the main trunk, was a bald eagle's eyrie. Eagles often chase ospreys who've just risen from the river with fish in their claws. The osprey, frightened, drops the fish, which the eagle catches before it hits the water. A nesting osprey will dive-bomb an eagle who, wary, chooses not to fight.

I'm probably corny when I say that I craved to see Gaea, that earth goddess. So, you see, I did pick up bits and pieces from those classes I dozed through in high school. Helpful hints in nature are there waiting for us, if we open our minds and hearts. Nature, as Walt Whitman said, is an open book. "Let whosoever will read and be enlightened read therein." Gaea, that cunt, was a no-show.

During these weeks I watched for clues—if I saw blue more than pink I'd have boys. If neither color topped the other, there'd be one of each. I'd strip and stand before Mom's bedroom mirror with the curved wood running along the sides and examine my body. My skin tone is white, almost pearly, and picks up sun tones. I've said that I guessed I'd have boys; yet I wanted girls, or at least one. So, as the sun played over my breasts, I'd wait to see pink hues before dressing again. The birthmark pig running across my belly was really stretched now, and, though no tits were visible, the critter was an adult.

My parents helped a lot, for they might have hated me for disgracing them. Besides, real whores like what they do, and, God knows, I had no fun in my one-time shot with Griffin. From now on, if men used their penises for nothing but peeing that would be just fine with me. Put all human sperm in banks. Let women inseminate themselves. Simple! Let men fuck sheep, does, or themselves . . . whatever turns them on. Just leave women alone.

My folks were church-goers—once in awhile—and were on the roster of the Christ Evangelical Church, turning up on holidays. They never condemned me; in fact, they seemed keyed up about the births. I was their celebrity. Through my kids they'd recapture their own lost youth. You can slap me for thinking this—I've wanted to many times myself. Say I'm selfish. I've got an ego. I admit it. I try to keep the short hairs clipped. Remember when my aunt was shot? As a suspect I felt both scared and important. We're not ants milling around a queen. We all want to stand out. And I was a flop at school, for I had never knuckled down, so couldn't go to college. Most high-school grads who do poorly get a diploma, a handshake, and the message: "Take care of yourself as best you can. You're not ready for college." That's why I tried to make something of my life and joined the Army. I could start over. Make it to the top. I've always had a furry monster on my chest, like that nightmare in Fuseli's picture. You showed it to me once in an art book. The poor bastard, though he's asleep, has a hard night; for his sheets are all twisted. On his chest sits this imp with eyes glowing like head-lamp eyes on a walleye pike. Why is it when we're victims the tormentors love it? Why can't they just fuck us over, if you'll excuse the expression, and let us get on with our lives? Oh, I never said life was a bowl of cherries. We may be itty-bitty-fishies in an itty-bitty-pool, and the baddies wait to suck us in. I tried, dammit, my whole life.

What needs facing up to is the sick joke—sick enough to raise nasty laughter in Heaven for a week—that someone like myself, hardly a card-board cut-out paper-doll image of a cheerleader, once she decides to find out what women get from screwing, who never thinks she'll get trapped, is trapped, as the mathematicians say, to the second power. I don't know enough about square roots. "Root" means "penis," right? Back then I sure was "square." Stuck with a kid after a ten-minute sex jam with a horny male? But two of 'em? That's justice?

Sure, my ovaries got hot. I guess you'd say that my ignorance of the male/female business was like putting a deposit in a bank for a rainy day? My hormones were earning interest; I hit the jackpot with one fuck, double bars. It might have been cherries, right?

So far as I know, Jane, who was twelve, was never teased about me in school. Marge was then living in Port Edwards in southern Wisconsin and was snotty about my plight. You, Bob, were always against our keeping the kids, and actually found a Chicago lawyer and his wife to adopt them. For a dozen years you washed your hands of me, of my kids, and of the folks for ignoring your advice. I don't think you've ever forgiven us. "We'll never give our own flesh and blood away," Dad vowed, meaning that all of your kids, in wedlock and out, must be kept and raised. I still think we did the right thing. True, Dad often teased me. "Nell," he'd say, "why do you make everything twice as hard on yourself as other people do? Wouldn't one kid be enough?"

I proved myself more of a woman than the local girls who chased tourists. By seducing one of these rich guys, they thought they'd marry and spin off to Chicago or Milwaukee to a life of wealth and pampering. This just popped into my head, something I never saw back then: if I did not fit the image of the cheerleader, I'd show 'em! This is one female who can produce!

As the days passed, I wanted the kids' births delayed so I'd be pampered longer, for I was Dad's "little girl." And even when he called me "the best of his boys," I melted like a chocolate bar in the sun. When I talked tough, he'd give me back the same and worse, and then to please him would soon have me acting age seven or eight. And Doc Barney helped. "Cocoa," he said, "We'll get 'em out of the oven in fine shape. Don't worry."

When we lived in Sundstein, Mom was a loner; but, in town, she was more gregarious. Whenever she got her hair fixed, she boasted of the forthcoming blessed event. She even persuaded me to get one of those tight-curl perms which has an almost 'Afro quality, which older ladies up here like. Mom had always sneered at unmarried pregnant local girls. She had such a way of freezing her chin you imagined old Savanorola, or whoever it was back in Italy, condemning sinners until they tied him to a stake and burned him. *Keeping Up Proprieties*— Mom was good at that, and it wasn't her attractive side. If you're going to judge others, you need a security net in case you fall from grace.

Once I was pregnant, Mom couldn't have been more helpful. "We're in this thing together, Nell," she'd comfort me. "We'll see it through."

Then Truth bared its fangs, showed its wolfish face, ready to pounce. The twins would flop forth. I brought on my lot, and my folks would eventually have to stand back and let me struggle. Until the actual births, I never imagined I'd be scraping shitty diapers, chaining my family to twenty-four-hour baby duty, wiping up sour milk, and trying to soothe screaming infants.

Normally, God was in Heaven and I was down here; all spun forth as He'd decreed. With all He had on his mind, how could He find time for me? I liked asking forgiveness and accepting the punishment God demanded (and every night I asked Him for forgiveness). If You must punish me, please, God, be kind! I liked the story of Christ on the cross—where he said that if God couldn't take the cup of suffering away, He, Christ, would drink it Himself! What else could I do?

One mid-afternoon, filled with thoughts of sin and pain, I walked through back streets, arriving at the Lutheran Church, which I knew would be open but empty of people. Back then, no churches were locked. You could even leave the communion plate on view.

As I approached the front steps, I saw Reverend Krubsack, his shirt sleeves drawn up by rubber bands, digging in his dahlias. When I was sure he wouldn't see me, I marched up the steps and into the church. There was an odor of stale choir robes, burnt candles, and lilacs— from a bouquet near the small pipe organ. Light filtered through the stained glass window showing Jesus with lambs in his arms, a sheep crook, and a blizzard of adoring sheep gazing up.

The front pew creaked when I sat down. Above the altar a pastel Jesus with girlish wrists, machine-carved from wood, held a beating heart topped by a gold tiara. On his free hand stigmata were visible. His blonde curly beard, and the wispy hair forming his mustache, were beautiful. I craved for Him to love me. When I offered Him my heart, I felt little meaty doors open and close and open, inviting Him in. I took deep breaths, sitting far back in the pew, accommodating my babes.

Then, as the tiny doors swung shut, they felt like ice. My anxious heart received nothing. I remained unfulfilled. "Please, Jesus," I prayed while my hands shook.

When I looked again at Jesus, His smile was sad. His eyes were dead polychrome wood. I guess I cried—you know, those sobs that start off a heavy weep-session? A few tremors, a choke or two in the throat, some mistiness at the eyes—and then the downpour. And I'd wet my pants!

I dashed outside, and to this day have never gone back to a Church for help of any kind. But at times I call on God's name. He's usually a nurturing breeze, or volcano lips spewing lava. Mountains forming in days of the batholiths when volcanic rock swelled into folds and crusts better suited what was happening to me than virgin births where angels breathe on your face as you bear Divine children. Better a beaver with a gnawed-off willow branch in its teeth than a cute little sexless creature wearing wings and a halo and bearing an olive branch. Which Annunciation would you prefer?

Twice the good Lord sent his handmaidens, Mrs. Ardell Spruce and her friend Madamia Frechette to visit Mom and me. Both of these biddies, the first scrawny, the second fat (her breasts flopped about under her arms), both in their fifties, were members of the Pioneer Fundamentalist Church, whose minister later preached bad sermons at both my father's and mother's funerals. Both of these women looked as though they'd spent the morning cleaning dirt from the far corners of their souls, then, after dousing themselves in lavender water, threw on stiff dresses with patent leather belts, and proceeded to the Lord's work, which meant checking on me, a miserable, lost sinner. Mrs. Spruce and Mom shared the same beauty parlor, the source of much town gossip. Mom served them coffee left over from that morning's brew, and a couple of glazed doughnuts. I knew by the way they shook the corners of their paper napkins they were up to no good. You can always smell the skunk oil coming from people bent on doing something for your "good."

When I turned to go to the living room, Mrs. Spruce chimed out, beckoning me back to the kitchen: "There are glorious wonders afoot. You should know all about that, Nell, since your folks brought you up to know the difference between good and evil." She took another sip of coffee and cleared her throat. "All children, no matter how de-formed, ugly, or miserable in the circumstances of their birth, are loved by the Lord Jesus."

"Yes, yes, He works in Mysterious Ways," Mrs. Frechette chimed in like a cheeping bird.

Mom rose from her chair and set about watering a pair of geraniums she was nursing until she could set them outside. I hoped she'd find a way to turn off the spigots these biddies set flowing. Their faces kept yakking at me from Bible pages.

"Dorothy," said Mrs. Spruce, moving forward on her chair, anxious to make a point, "I would never cast stones at your dear Nellie, but I do hope she'll join us Sunday. We'll pray on her behalf. The best Christians, and we count ourselves among 'em, must invite sinners into their embrace."

"We'll pray mightily," Mrs. Frechette promised. "Then she'll have her sin of being with child out of wedlock wiped off God's slate. There's nothing He can't forgive."

"Nell"—it was Mrs. Spruce's turn—"you don't look all that big. We'd heard that you'll have twins. Are you sure? And the daddy? Anyone we know? That Remington boy? You were dating him." She waited briefly for my reaction before she went on: "Maybe it was a soldier in the Army. . . ."

"I can't take any more of this," I muttered to Mom.

The women, momentarily taken aback, exchanged nervous smiles.

Mom opened the door, speeding them on their way. They left flipping their hands in frustration.

I hated pain, and at birth-time just knew I'd be reduced to snivelling and yelling. Yet, from all I'd heard, women during childbirth are supposed to scream and chew on their fists until they bleed. There's also supposed to be a scared future father in the picture, standing by your head, stroking your sweat-soaked tresses.

Mom tried her best to explain what was coming. "There'll be bad pains, and the head will come first, and you'll be soaked, and you'll hurt so much—I can't tell you. . . . But it will end, and you'll have your babies."

"Nellie," Dad said, "you'll take it like a man. I know you will." That was his prediction. I recall one of the deer hunts I made with him towards the end of my pregnancy.

The deer trail, hundreds of years old, crossed a tamarack swamp where the deer browsed, dropped their marble-sized scat, and moved on. They had no trouble keeping the trail open despite deep snows. Once they reached the north slope near our stand, flaring, snow-laden balsam and sugar maples, the latter too high up with snow for easy browsing, hid them from hunters. They ate balsam only when other trees were depleted of needles and leaves. With my rifle cocked I was to wait behind some spruce we had set up to conceal us from the deer. Dad would circle for a mile, perhaps more—you could easily travel over the hardened snow crust then—and follow his trail back, driving deer past my blind. Alert, I'd bag one.

I was bundled in long-johns, wool shirt, a mackinaw jacket and trousers, lined leather gloves, a cap with ear flaps, and a bit of stocking I drew across my mouth for additional warmth. Most vulnerable were my feet, which, despite wool socks and gum-rubber boots, would get so cold they'd lose feeling. Then you worried. I worked up a routine of stomping—without making enough noise to frighten the deer.

I remember feeling frozen—the sky had sun dogs, those frosty clouds shot through with teal and salmon sun rays, announcing a bitter cold spell. My eyebrows were frosted, and the face-piece drawn across my mouth was also frosted. I had just removed my right glove to blow on my fingers when I saw a ten-point buck, his body half-turned, his head facing me, a perfect target. I cocked the rifle, raised and aimed, but because my fingers were so cold, I misfired and the stock of the gun struck my cheekbone. I was sure I'd broken it. There was some blood. The buck, of course, sped off.

Dad heard the shot, hurried over, saw the blood on my face, and with his jackknife removed a flap of torn skin. "You were brave, Kiddo."

Quilts

To MAKE the first quilt I used a yard and a half of white muslin and a half-yard of yellow for a Mother Goose scene. I picked through Mom's scraps for pieces. One of Jane's books had a Mother Goose standing against a neutral background. After pinning a flattened paper grocery bag to the wall, I drew a Mother Goose sitting in a rocker, holding a book which said *Nursery Rhymes.* I've always liked to draw. On another bag, I sketched three goslings on a floor listening to Mother Goose read. Two goslings wear boys' jackets. The third wears a pinafore. I wanted to give the impression that the reading was happening inside a cozy room. A small braided rug would help. To make the rug, I folded inch-square pieces four times, and then began sewing them together as you would a rag rug, ending up with a nice oval. With black embroidery floss I ran threads to suggest walls. In one wall I put a window, also of floss. Of solid-stitch embroidery I made a small table holding a lamp. Using carbon paper I traced the patterns I needed. The rocking chair was of brown material. Mother Goose's sunbonnet was of red and white polka dots. The yellow cloth I'd purchased worked nicely for her body, and for the bodies of the goslings. The Nursery Rhyme book was blue with words embroidered in black thread to suggest the binding. The entire scene fit on the three-by-five-foot cloth, just the right size for a crib. To complete the picture, Mom used her sewing machine and surrounded each figure with buttonhole stitching, fastening each to the original muslin. Next, we cut an old quilt for a filler, and for the backing used some cotton material that had rabbits and squirrels all over it. To put the quilt together, I had to sew all three main pieces, inside out, on three sides, so that, once completed, the seams wouldn't show. Finally, I tied it by threading a darning needle with yarn, going down and up, leaving tails for making knots. Three inches over I repeated the maneuver. I tied each in a hard knot and snipped the thread, securing the quilt from slipping inside the filling. I turned and sewed the last edges. Some people put bindings on the quilt, but I don't.

"That's a great job, Nell," Mom said. "Now, if you want to start on the booties, I'll show you how to crochet them." She took out her hooks and yarn; but, despite her patience I never managed to get the hang of it, so gave up.

On the 11th of June, at 5 a.m., I was in the bathroom. "Mom," I shouted, "I can't stop peeing."

"Oh, my God," she exclaimed, "the water's broke."

Dad started the car while I threw a bathrobe around my shoulders, grabbed the suitcase I'd prepared, and sat in the back of the car on a blanket. By the time we reached St. Mary's Hospital in Rhinelander, the blanket was soaked. I expected I'd be back home in a couple of hours. I'd miss Doc Barney, for Eagle River doctors couldn't use the Rhinelander medical facilities for their patients.

With my parents waiting, I was prepped. A Dr. Wright was scheduled for the delivery. A nun asked if I planned to breast-feed. "No," I said. "As a single mother I'll have to work. So I can't be tied down."

"Good," she said.

At this point, I was not yet having pains. "They'll come," said the Franciscan nurse. "They'll come." She told the folks to go home, there wasn't much they could do.

I remained in an anteroom near the check-in station where the nun advised me to walk as much as possible. I got sick of looking down at my bedroom slippers with their bunny faces.

After six hours the spasms hit. When they were seven minutes apart I went into a labor room. Other than a picture of Jesus exposing his bloody heart, with a piece of dried palm leaf behind the frame, the ecru-toned room, as I remember, was bare, except for a narrow hospital bed on wheels, a table with water pitcher and basin, a chair with metal arms, and a buzzer.

No one had so far explained the mechanics of birth. Instead of pushing with the pain, I relaxed, which was the opposite of what I should do. When the pains were five minutes apart, the nun was there. "No, no, honey. Bear down. Pretend you're on the potty." Her voice soothed me, and her hands were warm on my face. "I'm Sister Theresa," she said. "I'll be with you." She took my pulse, timed the contractions, and said: "I'll be back in a few minutes."

I vowed not to come off weak. *Take it like a man.* Very ironic, right? I've boasted much to you of my private strength. Yet, while I won't equate feeling child-like with being female, women and children do share attitudes. Birthing women may turn back to their childhood, aching for a mother or a father (a husband might serve both these roles, but I doubt it) to soothe them. Men, if they had to give birth, would be babies, too, even more so. I do know that men are worse babies than we females ever are.

By 5:30 I was "fully dilated," with spasms now three minutes apart. Since no one had explained dilation, I had no idea what they were talking about. The new spasms began with an intense churning and knotting in my belly which eased only when I pushed against them. Shortly, I was in stirrups, strapped down, squeezing on metal grips. I was still not yelling, and did, I guess, amaze (and please) the nun, who later said that she had never seen a birth (let alone a double one) where the woman didn't scream.

Then, in a haze, I saw a man clad in white with a stethoscope around his neck. "Hi, Miss Peters. I'm Dr. Wright." He was medium height, ruddy, with a Ronald Colman mustache, and a set smile. "Everything's fine. I'll just slap these rubber gloves on and have a look."

He positioned himself on a chair in view of the area, i.e., the full scene of my bare butt hanging out, who knows with what assortment of juices oozing forth. I felt no modesty—any such feelings soaked like pee into sand earlier that day, during the poking, sniffing, and examining done by the nurses.

"OK, Miss Peters," the doctor cut in. "I see the first head. Bear down. That's good. Don't hold back. More. Here comes the head! There's the shoulders! It's a boy, Miss Peters! Number One."

"Michael David," I whispered. "He's Michael David."

"Now, here comes Number Two. Push. Push."

More pain as the second head shoved forth, followed swiftly by the rest of the body.

"It's another boy," said the doctor.

"David Michael," I told him. "David Michael."

Ejecting the placentas was almost as painful as the births. The nurse said I was lucky there was no curetting or stitching. Most women require both.

"Well, that's it." The doctor wiped my forehead with an icy cloth.

When Sister Theresa walked in with a baby on each arm, I held my sons for the first time. Not knowing which was David and which was Michael, I drew the flannel wrap away from the first face. "You sweetheart," I said. "You don't have freckles." The other face was also clear of them. I didn't know that freckles don't appear at birth. When I inspected their tummies there were no birthmark pigs.

The boys went back to the nursery, and wide tight bandaging was wound round my abdomen and over my breasts to keep them from enlarging. They were first wiped with substantial amounts of camphorated oil which the nurse said would also keep them down in size, since I would not be breast-feeding. Later that evening Dad and Mom appeared, relieved that I was OK. In four days I would go home.

Eagle River, Wisconsin
General Delivery

June 15, 1952

Dear Bill,

I have waited to write to you until now, after the birth of your two sons, David Michael and Michael David, on the 11th of this month, in the hospital at Rhinelander. Mother and boys are doing fine.

I did receive your cold letter, and rather than go to court to prove you are the dad, and to mess things up, I am counting on your good nature, Bill, to come up here and see your wonderful sons and marry me. As I said before, I don't expect to stay married very long, but even a few days would help the twins not have marks against them throughout their lives. It's the boys I'm worried about.

You said I'd been playing around. Bill, this is not true. I knew one man once, and you were that man.

The boys do resemble you a lot, and it's hard to tell one from the other. My folks are wonderful with them, sparing me. I will, though, have to go to work as soon as I can get out of bed, for I've used up my Army savings, and there is no other help—social welfare.

We can make a good life together. I know we can.
Nell

The preceding letter came back unclaimed, addressee unknown.

If my emotions strike you, reader, as different in any particulars from what you might have expected, that's understandable. I still feel a lot of guilt. The simple needs of daily life were enough to sink most new mothers—and grandparents.

The diapers alone were mountainous messes of runny doodoo and pee, and Mom's small washer never stopped churning. We bought a drier, which helped. Until then, I trundled the wet diapers down to the local laundromat and used their driers, which was not kosher, as they say. Within a month I was an employee there, making fifty cents an hour, and I could then freely use the facilities. Considering the poverty wage they paid, I had no qualms about this.

When I was working, obviously, the main care for the babies came from Mom and Dad. Fortunately, Dad was rarely busy in his shop, so could rock and feed the boys. One of my warmest images of Dad is of him sitting in that old rocker with a child in each arm singing them to sleep. I felt that while I gave him much grief, I also gave him joy.

7

David Michael and Michael David

⟨⟨⟨◦⟩⟩⟩

Y OU'LL HAVE to forgive me, Bro, if I take a break, for emotions are crowding in on me like a baby's fists beating my face. I woke too early, I guess, my head spinning with things to tell. It's your fault, getting me here while the frost is still on the pumpkin, as they say. Sure, we've done lots of work, and we want to finish before you fly home. I'm surprised we don't hate each other. Nobody's ever pulled stuff like this out of me before. What gets to me most is that our folks had to raise the twins. Mom had her kids spread over lots of years—so it wasn't fair to make her start a new family all over again.

Well, let's have another slug of your lousy coffee, and we'll get back to work. If you know pains are waitin' to ambush you, you might as well relax. That's always been my motto. And since life's already dumped a lot of crap on yours truly, I'm not afraid of what else might fall on my head. Oh, you have to pee again? I'm worried about you. The *prostrate* problem old men get? Okay, so go shake it. I'll give my teary eyes another wipe and be ready to go.

Hard Rain

⟨⟨⟨◦⟩⟩⟩

M Y FIRST JOB was at Siefert's laundry making fifty cents an hour, on the mangle, ironing table cloths and bed sheets for area resorts. Since the business was seasonal, on Labor Day I was laid off.

With the twins, Mom, Dad, and I were on call twenty-four hours a day. When one was down, the other was up. My room, a large closet, had space for a cot and a bassinet. Dad had the largest bedroom, so

133

the second bassinet was in there. Since his welding business was slow, he didn't seem to mind losing sleep. And he was up most nights racked with coughs from the emphysema he caught working in the shipyard.

I tried to care for the boys in the wee hours, although I had to be at the laundry at 8 a.m. I needed that job, for after paying the hospital and doctor bills, and buying eight dozen diapers, I was broke. A small sum came from what was called 52-20, where for a year veterans received twenty dollars per week for adjusting to civilian life. Dad had no regular income. Though I knew that laundry work was seasonal, I was still surprised to be laid off, thinking that if I worked hard I'd be hired year-round. That didn't happen. I also worried that Janie, now twelve, because of the twins, faced psychological problems. I understood her wanting to leave home, and I felt guilty about that, too, for I never realized how destructive the twins were on her. Only when Janie and I visited you in California a dozen years ago, in our chats, did I realize the scope of my parents', Janie's, and the twins' ordeals.

Collecting Junk

AFTER MY laundry job ended I spent more time with my sons. Although Mom later fussed, at this time she behaved like the real mother. To give up my rights was easy. I guess I was weak.

I helped Dad scavenge the Lincoln dump for metals. The dump, a mile south, was on a marsh fill. At any time after 3 p.m., collecting was good, for by then that day's refuse was all there. I drove Dad's Chevie pickup which, like most of his make-do vehicles and tools, was lousy. There was no ignition key. You sparked it through an extension cord run from the battery to the starter and taped to the steering wheel. By pushing two prongs together, one negative and one positive, the engine kicked in. There was always a body jolt, but not one you couldn't handle. To stop the car, you held the cord against the metal of the steering wheel, shorting the vehicle. For cold weather, Dad installed another battery below the first one. You hooked up the second from inside the cab, which in turn hooked to the first, providing the juice. Once the car was running, you disconnected the second battery.

Dad was a poor man's Thomas Alva Edison. He invented a fork fit with welding tines for probing discards. We scavenged aluminum lawn chairs, burnt-out washers, grinders, and car armatures. Best were old refrigerators, for they yielded ten pounds of nice clean copper. If the motors were sealed, Dad burned them open with his acetylene torch. Copper was the best metal for resale. We also collected car wheels, and any pieces of iron good for welding.

Dad's specialty was flower planters. He'd start with an old well point, an iron shaft about four feet long for driving into the ground, to which he'd weld curved forks taken from old hay rakes. These gave the exact turn he needed for hanging flower holders. The holders he made from auto head lamps, drilling holes in the bottom of each for drainage. For other planters, he welded discarded iron for holding clay flower pots. He either sold these for ten bucks or gave them away.

Now's the time to describe his welding shop, his main source of income, where I tried helping him make money.

The building, of cinder blocks, was about twelve feet square, and sat fifty yards from the house. There was one window and a pull-up door so that a car or truck could drive in for repairs. The window overlooked a swamp. A small sliding door faced the highway. Visible from the street was a metal Coca-Cola sign, painted white, with shaky black letters announcing "SAM'S WELDING." This Dad hung by tire chains from a welded frame. His notion was that if the sign swung in the wind, it's flash would attract customers.

He never got around to installing a floor. For heat he split two oil barrels with his acetylene torch, and set one on top of the other. One half-barrel he filled with waste oil drained from cars (collected from local garages). This dripped slowly through copper piping into a lower half-barrel. If we needed more heat, he turned off the pet-cock and stopped the oil. Through a door in the bottom barrel, he burned wood.

He owned both an acetylene torch and an arc welder. He could throw the torch and tanks into the back of his truck and travel to a job. The arc welder stayed in place. Somehow, despite his coughing and stomach cancer he made enough to pay for torches and bottled gas. The shop was dark, greasy, and smoky. On blackened shelves sooty tools lay. Many of these Dad invented, including a complex system of welded metal straps and quivers for transporting welding tanks to outside jobs. The far west corner of the shop he reserved for peeing.

Most mornings, his health permitting, he was in the shop by 6 a.m., no matter how extreme the weather. He got his fires roaring, threw on his welding helmet, and worked. A lousy business man, he never charged enough. He loathed bosses. His shop was his life-long dream of being self-employed. As you've seen by now, I'm a lot like him.

Fleshing Mink

ANOTHER SEASONAL JOB lasted most of November. At least I'd have money for Christmas. Frederickson's Mink Ranch, a mile south of town, prepared its animals for market soon after the pelts reached their best color, pile, and gloss. Locals complained of the stench floating from the wire pens. The only thing like it—and mink stench was far worse—were sulphurous paper mill fumes coming from Rhinelander.

Our jobs, starting at 8 a.m., lasted for eight hours. We sat on cobbler's benches where the shoe last was an oak prong about three feet high for stretching pelts. On the top V the creature's head was impaled. Near its base it widened to nearly a foot. The hides were sorted into silver, black, and brown. The first two were the more expensive breeds.

The pelts, having been skinned the night before, were piled in tubs of water until they reached room temperature, which was necessary for a good fleshing. The skinning, speedy, was performed by slaughterers in another building who simply yanked off the hide after first slitting the tail lengthwise. Then they removed the feet at the joint, keeping the head intact. With a quick jerk the hide yanked free.

A stripped carcass looked this way: you first saw the eyes, the nose with cartilage still intact, and the nostril holes, chin, and teeth. The males always fleshed more easily, for the females had prominent teat holes. You grabbed a pelt from the tub, slipped the head over the top of the wooden spike, and draped the rest of the hide. Since the strippers had yanked the hides off inside out, you faced a mass of tallowy inner hide, streaked with gobs of flesh, blood, and fat.

Our fleshing instrument resembled a drawing knife used by loggers for stripping tree bark. It had to be dull, otherwise we'd slice the hide. Starting near the head, with one hand on either side of the knife you drew the blade down. Smelly grease dripped along your arms, so that you often had to wipe yourself. When one animal was done, you fit it onto a free board half an inch thick, the size of a mink. We first put a tack through the lip to fasten down the pelt, then, after stretching it tight, we hammered tacks into the out-turned legs, also tightening the pelt along the sides. Next we turned the board over, brought the tail, which we had already "gutted" of caudal bones, up. To keep the tail from shriveling, and in order for it to "cure" right, we used care in tacking down the tail. Once a few pelts were done, a boy took them, initialed your boards, and carried them off to a room where they were hung on hooks to be wiped twice a day for a week. I received a quarter for each pelt, and on good days worked thirty pelts. The four of us, by the end of the month, had processed about three thousand pelts. My salary was somewhere between twenty-five and forty dollars per week, which for northern Wisconsin was good. Remember, my take-home pay from the laundry was about twenty-two dollars, so things were looking up.

I fleshed mink for three more seasons.

Butchering

MUCH OF OUR food came from butchering during the early winter snows. You had to be sure the meat would stay frozen up on the roof away from dogs and coyotes. The first time I helped butcher, the morning was blizzardy with scraps of sun peeking through boiling snow clouds. The boar and his sow were as usual squealing for mash. We kept a covered pair of steel oil drums near the sty which we filled with soured slops from the house, mixed with bran chaff, oats, and ground corn bought in hundred-pound bags from Morgan's Feed. When our hens were ranging free, we had to keep the barrels covered, for the stupid birds, anxious to eat the grain floating in the swill, slipped in and drowned. These birds we simply fed to the pigs.

That morning Dad chopped through a good two inches of ice covering the swill to reach soft mash. We'd also mixed swill with hot water in the house, so that the trough was soon steaming. Anxious to eat, the hogs thrust their snouts clear to the bottom, scooped up food and threw back their heads with their piggy pink eyes, swallowing. When the boar's head was deep in the mash, Dad brought his rifle to the skull. The boar fell into the trough, then slipped to the icy ground and lay on his side, throbbing.

Pigs sound exactly like humans in distress. Also, there's something human about how their eyelashes look. And I know how pigs feel!

Since Dad was squeamish about slitting throats, that was Everett's job. Using a sharp knife, once they had dragged the body half-way out of the pen, Everett sliced the suety throat. Since Mom disliked blood sausage, and though Dad loved it, he gave in to Mom and let the protein-rich fluid seep into the snow.

We dragged the pig along the ice to a frame beneath which a fire blazed under a big oil barrel filled with water, ashes, and lye. Using a block and tackle, after severing the head, we hoisted the boar by his back legs, plunging him a dozen times into the barrel. Removing the barrel and dousing the fire, we set to work with a pig-scraper, brushes, and knives, removing all hair, which came off fast because of the lye.

The head, considered by some people a delicacy for head cheese, we fed to the dogs. By mid-afternoon, the butchering over, Dad and Everett carved chops and roasts, and Mom rendered the fat into lard. We pickled the feet, which Dad and I loved.

As winter deepened we ice-fished a lot. Occasionally, neighbors who couldn't pay Dad in cash for welding jobs brought him fish and venison. One afternoon, Jerry Busher appeared in his panel truck, backing right up to Dad's overhead doors. "Sam," he said. "I've got something. This animal had a heart attack in my front yard. It's not deer season, so I've got to get rid of it. Thought you could use the meat."

With Dad's help Jerry eased the gutted animal from his truck and onto some flattened cardboard boxes. When Jerry left, we hung the carcass from the rafters and shucked off its hide. The meat looked juicy, fatless, and had a soft purple stain which always meant sweet flesh. This had been a great winter for deer—there was browse, so there were no horror stories of herds starving, nibbling on spiny, nearly indigestible balsam branches, to live.

Once dad had butchered the deer into loin, haunch, and rib portions, he turned to me. "Well, the rest is yours, Kiddo."

I sliced chops, steaks, and roasts, and ground up hamburger. While the twins were not yet able to chew venison, they loved the gravy I stirred into their mashed potatoes. Since baby food was costly, by the time the boys were six months old we fed them almost everything we ate. And, like beef, venison could be pureed. The boys grew fast, and I made sure they received daily vitamins. Mom fed them bottles of whole milk sweetened with Karo syrup, which is what she'd fed us. I couldn't talk her out of those calories.

Cranberries

THE COMMERCIAL CRANBERRY, grown on bog farms, differs from the wild fruit in marshes (like those surrounding Minnow Lake) which speckles like a robin's egg then turns bright red and dangles into the water where it grows. These are Small Cranberries, a creeping shrub with oval leaves white on their under sides. The pink flowers have protruding stamens. The Large Cranberry, the cultivated shrub, differs, and has long, clumsy-looking, forked stems with lots of branches. The leaves are like spruce needles, sharp and leathery. The stems where the berries grow have no leaves and form hard angles to the main branch. At harvest time, spraying the bogs with poisons kills both rodents and nearly all plant life, including the cranberry bushes. Only the berries stay glued to the stems. At this point growers flood the marshes, floating the berries. Machines with big scoops scrape up the fruit, loading it onto conveyer belts running straight to processing. Inside, as berries tumble through flowing water, we women had to sort out all the debris we could, which included dead mice, frogs, deer and rabbit scat, and scraps of wood. Since scat was plentiful, some got through. The joke was: "Just add more sugar and you won't taste the scat." Big steel cookers turned the berries into sauce. Our starched, sanitary, white uniforms were a contrast to what ended up in the food.

When the processing plant opened in 1953 I was one of the first in line for a job. For eight hours a day, for a dollar and a half an hour, without benefits, my job was to take the pint-sized cans as they rolled off the washer assembly line and place them on the canner belt. The cans, as they rolled forward, were squirted full of fruit. After sealing and another washing, they were labeled.

Since this job was also seasonal, no matter how hard you worked, there were no permanent jobs. The plant which once ran year round, twenty-four hours per day, is closed now, preferring to fold rather than pay the large fines environment officials levied for their poisoning the waters in which the cranberries grew. In the mindless routine of this job, I would see the faces of my boys trapped in those empty cans, swirling away from me.

House-Moving

—◦/◦/◦—

IN 1954, EVERETT married his second wife Barbara and worked for a contractor moving old houses. During summer weekends, I helped him; so he made up for some of the nasty things he did when we were kids. He now even seemed concerned about my boys.

I shovelled gravel, poured cement, and carried blocks for house foundations. My on-the-job training with Dad when he built our basement helped. Everett rented a cement mixer, where you simply threw in dry cement and water and pulled a switch. Once the foundation dried, a house was moved in on rollers and pushed up on the new foundation, which was incomplete on one side so that the house could be shifted easily into place. Then we finished the last wall. The pay was good: two-fifty an hour with no taxes. Like most of my jobs, this one, too, flew off with the cold weather.

Punching up the System

W E SURVIVED by learning how to milk the system, including welfare. While Dad was almost always honest, he shared the working-class ethic that justified beating the system, short of committing a felony. He poached the occasional deer, for we needed the meat, which Mom canned in Mason jars and hid in the cellar under the living room floor. Also, Dad hooked bass and walleyes out of season, exceeded bag limits, and kept undersized fish. When he ice-fished he erected a spruce tree shelter, chopped ice-holes with an axe, dropped lines baited with salted minnows, and hung warning flags shaped like fish hewn from bits of pine. A few yards off he piled more chopped spruce trees, mounded snow over them, and hid his illegal catch. At the end of the day, during the hour hike through the tamaracks back to our car, he'd think animal noises were game warden footsteps.

A frequent poacher was George Fetts, the red-haired, lanky "Squaw Man" I mentioned earlier, who had eleven kids. As soon as one sibling was too old for welfare, Mrs. Fetts ingeniously spewed forth another, maintaining a flow of welfare kids. The family was often in distress, and when Fetts was thrown in jail for poaching he knew that the county would feed his family. Tiring of Fetts's ploy, the sheriff released him to start his shenanigans all over again.

Once when Dad was working for forty dollars per month on a Works Progress Administration road crew, he stole a dozen sticks of dynamite. He showed me where he buried them, for he wanted to be sure that none of us stumbled onto the spot and blew ourselves up. The stuff was for blasting a hole for a basement.

True, the WPA program, and the HOLC, the Home Owners' Loan Corporation, through which we bought our new forty and built a house, were designed to assist poor folks. Did it make us too dependent? The system was like a rubber band that would never snap in your face.

Bob, you do remember those six sisters, the Mackeys, area legends, the "bearded ladies," who thrived on welfare and other handouts? One so obese that cascades of fat tumbled down her short dark body and kept a doctor from repairing her hernia. Her bowels had split through her stomach wall, and, while this slowed her walking, did nothing to slow her torrent of words. One sister, not quite as fat, had a squinting left eye, and by tilting her head to the right to see better, gave the impression of a Mrs. Tiggywinkle, though without the frilly bonnet. A grayish beard sprouted beneath her nose, surrounded her gray lips, and covered the rest of her face and her throat, disappearing onto her chest, only partly visible beneath a checkered wool shirt.

The Mackeys were a pioneer family, and these brotherless girls labored at farm chores, including milking cows and goats, shearing sheep, making soap and tilling, reaping, and sowing crops. Now, with the parents and half of the sisters dead, this trio remained welfare addicts. Monthly they visited a local church where clothes were piled up, free for the taking. They made the circuit of free-food pantries. Playing fair meant that you visited no more than two of these; but the Mackey sisters boasted to me of going eight times minimum. Their log house was crammed with unopened tins of canned fruits, juices, and vegetables, and packages of powdered milk, crackers, and cookies. Their acquisitiveness, an addiction, was characteristic of citizens hooked on welfare, much as a hospital patient is hooked to an intravenous life-support system.

Yes, I sure worked the system, and for lots of years. When my twins were young no programs helped single women raise kids. So once support came through I took advantage of all I could. No more empty pantries. When the folks adopted the boys legally, they got all the aid denied to me as a single mother.

I suppose some of my—let's call it playing Mother Hubbard— comes from my folks, who believed that since they'd paid taxes for years they deserved money flowing back—the County owed them that. In my case, I've paid premiums for years. One woman's teen-age son pegged a stone through her window, just hard enough to break it; it looked as if somebody had tossed it from a car. Her insurance company installed beautiful thermal panes, which lowered her heating bills. Now that's really using your imagination to rob the rich and pay the poor, don't you think?

I've not traveled much, so can't say what goes on in the rest of the country, whether doles encourage people to sit back, take food stamps and child welfare, and avoid working. You make your own scam. The sky's the limit. Sure, taxpayers in the end foot the bill. But let them that can pay, and them that can't take. An unmarried niece is being paid by the state to learn computers at a vocational school while the man who's sponged on her for years spends his time at home watching TV, drinking, and waiting for her to come home to him and their spoiled brat. He sometimes beats her. His family has always lived on welfare.

Where do I fit in all this? Who knows? We all take shortcuts, right? Even you do, Bob, if you'd tell the truth. Every worker in every store, restaurant, or office carries home stuff. Businesses allow for this. It's called *tret,* what butchers trim from steaks. It's an important part of surviving in the Northwoods.

Two Hearts That Beat as One

BY THE END of their second year, the boys blocked out mixed signals from adults. They now felt little pain, or they sure didn't show it if they did. They'd been so sweet, I had no idea this would happen—both my folks and I were to blame. Mom and Dad corrected them all the time, and when I was home so did I. We shouted at them, like I shout at Shadow. You grow up bellowing to get your points across and set standards. Jane also corrected the kids, and Everett was bad-tempered.

One evening, Mike tossed a baseball and hit some family pictures on an end table. The photos flew to the floor and smashed. I was tired, just having come home from work, so I grabbed Mike, dropped his pants, and was set to whip him when Mom rushed over. "Poor Mikey," she said. "He didn't mean it." Dad chimed in: "Don't whip my boy."

While my folks meant well, they were stressed by all the ugly demands. They were basically good people. While they never said (at least within my hearing) that they wished the boys weren't born, they came close. At one point, when the boys were in the sixth grade and Mom and Dad were sick of the boys' fighting each other, Dad thought a night in jail would cool them off! So he phoned the sheriff. The boys exploited Mom. She kept her true feelings to herself more than Dad. But Dad, as I've noted, already had both cancer and emphysema. Peace and quiet, not scrapping kids, was what he needed. Though Mom was stuck inside that house (Dad never finished building it), in her way she loved her grandsons.

I was blind to what was really happening, or maybe I chose not to see. When Mike or Dave were punished, their little bodies cramped up and their faces went blank. Their lives drained into icy looks. Lumps of glaring stone. Scary. All commands, criticizing, and threatened blows now struck a force-field inches from their bodies. Even when Dad whipped them with a belt they wouldn't cry. The teachers complained of their passive hatred; they were worse this way than any kids they'd ever seen.

I don't want to make monsters out of them; they could be pleasant and did help Mom with house chores and cleaned their room.

Adults go crazy when they're opposed, and though I didn't admit it then, and don't want to today, my folks and I often shot past our limits. When the kids even cooked up private lingo, which simply pissed us more, the physical abuse increased. A law of the universe went like this: punishing a child works contrary to the results you want—the more you punish the less effective you are. When you reach zero, the only impact is on the adults; your arm muscles get stronger from whipping the kid. There's no bad exercise, right?

Winters were the worst, for the boys were inside all day. They seemed to like school, away from our straps, belts, and shouts. I could have been more feminine, softer; my orders sounded like Dad's when he shouted. I don't know. Kids are not Shadows. Mine simply gave up listening.

Once they'd blocked us, we'd mix our signals, switching from soothing them to physical punishment and verbal abuse. We gave them clothes and toys. Books didn't count for much, although at first they liked being read to, especially by their Aunt Janie. Mike was lousy at school. Dave was better. He actually made it to Junior College and took up ecology. He's never found a job in the field.

I'm still baffled by the worlds of my boys. Total hostility? That seemed like their pure hatred melted you. When they turned numb, did their little brains short their synapses? You could have pinched them or drawn blood or flung them into a corner. They never cried even when the pain was bad. Here's an easy explanation: they sensed that through playing possum they could dominate their tormentors.

The kids were on my mind every day whether I was working at some mindless, cheap job or whether I was home. Should I, as you urged, have put them up for adoption? Maybe they'd be doctors or lawyers today. Was I weak for staying with my folks? Alone, how could I have supported myself and them? There are no pat answers. During their first years, I had no social life. I never went to bars, seldom to movies, and I certainly never dated, although I knew that I'd have to snag a man to look after me and them. And I had no car.

Would there be a man out there?

The Big Blonde Husband

"PERSIAN NIGHTS" perches on a rise where the Eagle and Wisconsin Rivers meet. The parking area sits fifteen-feet above the water, with marking posts placed at intervals just wide enough for a car to get through. Rumors say that some drunks, leaving the "Nights," have driven over the edge. I don't know of anyone who drowned, for there's no drop-off until you're out in mid-stream. Just some broken axles, knees, and sore heads. "If you wanna drink in here, you gotta take risks," the owner, Kitty Dean, always says.

Kitty—I don't think you ever met her—was a plump, aging, chain-smoker with long brunette hair. If she liked you, she'd lift up her tresses and show you where one of her husbands (he wasn't an Eagle Riverite, she said, for males here are "gents") bashed her during a brawl. In her teens, as the daughter of a Grand Ole Opry star, she herself had a career going, but dropped it after WW II when some of the Opry stars came back from Europe and Asia and decided that since they didn't like her mom they didn't like her either. She'd had it, and so had her three-member guitar and banjo band, the River Rats. Nobody, except for a few sots, came to hear her, wallowing in the indirect glow of her famous mom. Her mother, who used to fish and vacation in the Northwoods, bought her the "Persian Nights." Kitty allowed nothing on her juke box but her mother's hits, along with a few Charley Pride spinners. She boasted that her "establishment" was for down-and-outers, "welfare drinkers," late middle-aged men escaping their wives. "I've no qualms, Pussy Cat, about their spending their kids' milk money in here."

To the funky decor she inherited with the bar—an assortment of mounted ducks, bass, and a four-foot musky now crumbling into desuetude, its eyes having dropped out, and the shellac on its body peeling like bits of yellowish mica—she added her own touches. Like me with my garage sales, she kept everything. She'd spruce the tavern up with plastic flowers, frilly curtains, and gravity birds bopping their heads into beer mugs. I loved the flower arrangement she set into a gnarled cedar root resembling a gaping vagina: here she thrust plastic orchids, calla lilies, and irises, surrounding the lips with dried moss, giving the effect of pubic hair. Her "regulars" dumped beer dregs into the "pussy" and threw in dimes. Another item was a primitive painting, roughly four by three feet, of a winter landscape showing a man leaving a cabin to cross a field to a spruce forest where a buck and doe wait. The painter, "Myron Skeet," had chopped white pine poles into lengths, split them, bolted them together in a crude frame, and given them a Mylar gloss.

There was just room enough at the bar for half a dozen stools and a pair of naugahyde booths from pre-World War II days. The ceiling of hand-hewn pine timbers sagged, so that anyone over six feet tall had to stoop. If you asked Kitty why she named the place "Persian Nights," for nothing whatsoever hinted at the Oriental, not even a cat, she explained that only one of the half-dozen songs her Mom helped her record had that title. "It keeps remindin' me I'm a flop," she'd laugh. "Pleases Mom." Where she pumped beer was a fully-shaped Christmas tree about three feet high, trimmed with winking fireflies, which was on display year round. They, the lights, reminded her of Disneyland, and her favorite attraction, the "Pirates of the Caribbean," where you ride through a fire-fly Bayou scene.

"Persian Nights" was unique among town bars. The patrons were overall-clad hairy men with nicknames like "Clincher," "Fish Breath," "Viking," "Chain Saw," and "Slow Motor." You found the more upscale bars for Yuppies and tourists favoring piano show tunes and rib-eye steaks at resorts along the famous Chain-of-Lakes. There you'd get frosted beer mugs, imported ales, a choice of wines, and mixed drinks with fancy names like "Pina Colada Swizzle Express." In the "Nights" the common Friday fare was the Fish Fry. You think the fish came from local lakes? Wrong! It came from Iceland!

Here, Bob, at the "Persian Nights," I met Waino Kovisto.

Kovisto's red-haired sister Irene ran a run-down motel called E-Z REST across the highway from Dad's shop, and when she'd see the twins outside she'd come over and chat. On this morning, I brought the boys in their buggy so I could help Dad weld a broken plow.

Irene was the spitting image of the actress Celeste Holm, only shorter and skinnier, which is to say that in a Betty Grable movie she'd have helped her brother John Payne hook Grable. Irene never married. "Nell," she'd say, forming spit in the corner of her mouth: "There's no good man. Even a dead one is bad news. The only man I'd consider is your pa there, and I'd have to scrub him up first."

"What's a little blacksmith soot and car grease if you're horny, Irene?" I asked. "Dad looks pretty good."

Dad stopped pounding metal and came over.

"I like Finns, being one myself," Irene went on, tossing her head. "There's no way, Sam, you'd come out Finn white, even if I took a scrub brush to you."

"You won't try," Sam joshed. "Anyhow, you'd never be able to make a German like me look like a Finn."

Irene gave him the finger, then stood watching Dad finish welding.

Finally, Dad looked up: "Irene. Take Nell for a Bud. She's not been out of here in weeks. I'll treat."

"I've asked her before, Sam, lots of times. But she won't go."

"She needs to get away," said Dad, pulling out his wallet and giving Irene a fiver. "Here, go treat yourselves. I'll baby-sit."

Irene was one of the rare "Persian Nights" female regulars. I knew she drank a lot. Skinny blonde women who wrap their lips around beer bottles and chain smoke at the same time have a way of pursing their mouths. If you look close you'll see that those lips don't divide in the middle, and almost stick together at the sides, leaving the central part open for sucking in beer. My theory is that cigarettes make their mouths hot so they flush the feeling with ice-cold brew. Dribs of skin puckered Irene's cheekbones, aging them before their time.

There were three men in the bar, no women, and an old fat dog, Cookie, a grayish beagle whose body nearly touched the floor. She had legs like those splayed under fancy furniture. She ambled around sniffing. She actually looked moth-eaten, as though her head was once stuffed and mounted, the taxidermist gluing her lips in a perma-nent smile of bliss. She sweetly whimpered until you took up her proffered paw.

While I greeted Cookie, Irene traded insults with Kitty the owner, who was wearing a lonesome peacock feather in her hair, drawn into a bun. She served us beers, then drew us over to a couple of men.

"Nell, these are my cousins Balsam and Fish Dick, the Pietila brothers."

Balsam was a muscular freckled man about thirty in bib overalls with a sweat shirt showing Smokey the Bear peeing against a tree, advertising Bear Whizz Beer. Since the evening was warm, rare for August, Fish Dick was shirtless, his slim Nordic body a vivid contrast to his orange-red hair which was growing back from having been cut in an Iroquois style. His brown eyes took in things with amazing speed.

Balsam was one of a new kind of woodsman, who, equipped with chain saw, lineman's belt, protective helmet and gloves, shinnied up trees, lopped limbs, and, after securing tops to a strong rope dropped to the ground, tied the tree to another tree to mark the line of fall, and saw the original tree down. He was said to be the fastest man in the woods.

Fish Dick fished year round, and he always got his buck. He pre-ferred bow-and-arrow hunting, a controversial sport, for bad hunters would shaft a deer, leaving it to run for miles until it bled to death. Fish Dick lived by cutting timber with Balsam and by laying carpet and tile. His aim was to save money for some acreage and a one-man cabin where he could roam, hunt, and absorb Nature. He was rare up here, for in his late teens he had fought alcoholism and, without any official help, he cold-cocked the addiction. He still enjoyed bars, but drank cokes and non-alcoholic beer. His nickname came from an older woman he lived with during his boozing day who bragged (so she told his mom) that he shot such loads that if he were a buck walleye during spawning season he could fertilize a lake.

I edged over to the brothers, and on the way noticed another guy in one of the Naugahyde booths slumped over a table. He was blonde, as Scandinavians usually are, and had knocked over a bottle of beer, which drained over his knees. "What a mess," I thought, and turned to the Pietila boys. "Greetings, guys," I said. "How are they hangin'?"

"Thought you was a Flatlander," said Fish Dick, an insult he used on summer tourists.

"You got it wrong, Kid." I pretended to drop cigarette ash into his drink. "I could be your mother twice over."

"I've seen you pushing a buggy around town," Balsam chimed in. "How many kids you got in there? Three or four? Starting a school?"

"You insultin' this biddy, or what?"

"Them's her tots," Irene interposed. "Thought the whole town knew the story. You guys too busy playing with your Finn navels you can't see past 'em?"

"Gettin' any these days, Nellie?" Fish Dick asked with a wise-ass grin.

"I'll wipe your mouth out with pickerel shit," I retorted. "Or maybe loon shit; there's more of it. You're as crazy as a loon."

Balsam, laughing, did not take sides. Fish Dick was always good for a laugh. If you were hunting with him, he'd trip through the woods like a Chippewa. "You can't see no animals," he'd say, "unless you're still. Walk on the balls of your feet."

A groan as the drunk in the booth reared back, pounding the table. "Sis. Sis."

"It's your wiped-out brother, Irene," said Fish Dick. "Change his diapers."

I followed her to the booth.

"Name's Waino," said the guy, peering up through an amber stupor. Then he sank back. When he tried to light a cigarette, he hit the wrong side of his mouth with the flaming match.

"Here," I said, taking the match.

He forced open his eyes as though they were glued. The lashes were orange against his white forehead. Though he didn't look much past thirty-five, he was losing his hair, which was combed back on each side of his scalp.

"Who are you?" he demanded, brushing his freckled hand across the table, pushing at dead flies.

"Waino," Irene said, "let's go home."

"No."

"Take his arm, Nell. We'll drag him out of here."

When he launched a shadow-boxing rounder, I gave his forearm a quick twist. "We do feel sorry for ourselves, don't we?"

We got Waino out the door, dumped him into the back of Irene's car, and drove him home, Irene depositing me at Dad's on the way. My first night out was not a success—frustrating, yes; for the outing left me hanging.

A week later I was pumping air into Dad's forge, helping him slice some iron. The twins were near the door sitting at opposite ends of their buggy, banging stuffed rabbits together. I hadn't showered that morning—it was now about 3 p.m. My hair, though I recently had it curled, was a mess—you know, where the twists feel glued with grease and sand, and your scalp crawls? I was bra-less beneath a cheap T-shirt. I couldn't bend over or turn sideways without the damn things jiggling. In short, I was about as sexy as an angleworm cut in half trying to get itself together so it can keep on mating.

I looked up and saw him in the open doorway. Even if I'd wanted to run, I'd have to brush past him.

"Hi," he said, walking into the shop. Dad was flattening a rod for tightening the rear-end assembly of an old Model A used for hauling logs.

"How you doin', Waino?"

"Can't complain. Thought I'd see what Nellie was up to."

He was handsome standing there in tan gabardines with an open-throat, checked, short-sleeved shirt. He'd looked so fucked up in the "Persian Nights." He kept flexing his fingers, whitening the knuckles, a gesture I liked, for it said he was vulnerable. Not that his voice was shy; it was gruff, his "o's" stretched and dropped in a Wisconsin twang that came from immigrants meshing fractured English with regular English, like the "out" and "about" of Canadians.

I felt like saying I wasn't receiving visitors that day. I was a ninny standing there.

He greeted the twins with the usual chin-chucking that adults use, which babies must hate. Mike suddenly let out a scream, followed at once by Dave. The shop rang. There was no quieting them until I pushed the buggy outside, out of Kovisto's range.

"Nell, I apologize for the other night." I caught a whiff of pine-scented after-shave. Was he saying he needed me? I've always been a sucker when you signal that you can't get on unless I supply an extra oar. I was born, tempered, designed (or whatever other word you want) to be useful. I'm not perfect . . . don't get me wrong . . . but I perform good under other people's stresses, but not so good under my own. You, Bob, say my ego shrinks my eyeballs down to crawfish eyeballs. Don't I have any self except through other people? It scares me.

"I want to treat you," Waino said.

"What've you got in mind?" I asked.

"To take you fishing. The boys can come along. I know where the bass are biting. I'll bring the food. We'll have a picnic."

"The boys won't sit still," I warned.

"I want to take them. Bring out the father instinct." He touched the wicker hood of the buggy. "Tomorrow at ten? I'll bring the mosquito lotion."

The Picnic

B Y BACKING his trailer into the water, until the fringe of hard-packed sand gave way to soft muck and the wheels were up to the hub caps, Kovisto launched his fiberglass boat. We had driven in through Ewald's farm and along a road crossing the dairy and rolling down to Mud Minnow Lake. Our former land was directly across the water. The new owners had a boat and motor tied up near a cedar pole dock.

I had dressed the twins, who were now almost two, in cute overall outfits decorated with cinnamon bears balancing balls on their noses. Each wore a long-sleeved button-up pale blue sweater, for the day was chilly. Each baby wore a new cap with visor.

The mosquitoes were thick, although, as usual, perhaps because they were so big, they were slow enough you could smash them before they bit you. The venom did not cause the itching; the sting did.

We climbed into the boat, with Waino oaring. I was in the rear. Both boys were strapped into infant carry-on seats. Mike sat beside me. Dave I propped against Waino's seat. The food sacks were up front, except for the zipper tote bag with the kids' milk, juice, and diapers.

Waino baited poles with shiner minnows and began rowing slowly through some lilies. A fresh breeze now kept the mosquitoes down. Blue dragon flies mated in mid-air. Water bugs looking like Daddy Long Legs climbed around on lily pads. Bull frogs croaked. I grabbed a lily blossom. The aroma was delicate, like lilac with almond. In another hour, the flowers would close, avoiding the sun, to open later in the day once afternoon shadows covered the lake. The twins ripped off the lily petals, and for a good ten minutes were amused.

Waino's plan was to cast where bass waited to snag water insects foolish enough to drop from the big green pads into the lake. Waino would row a few yards, drop anchor, cast, then draw up the anchor, go a few yards north, and then do the same thing over again.

I tried to keep the twins happy, for talking and oar splashing kept bass from biting. The rocking boat lulled the kids and, miracle, they nodded off. They almost never slept at the same time. I was free to make casts.

The first bass struck. Unlike crappies and perch who nuzzle bait then strike, bass are so quick you either hook them or you don't. Mine, a four-pound small mouth, spun out numerous feet of line racing for deep water. I reeled in to set the hook, and to give tension, tiring him. (Odd, don't you think, that we see fish as male? Certainly, except during spawning when males go crazy over females and throng near the shores when the females come in to feed, you catch as many females, often roe-laden ones, as you do males. Also, patches of sperm give the impression of male-dominated waters. Draw your own conclusions.)

I drew the bass up alongside the boat so that Waino could reach over and flop him, slapping, into the boat. "That's a big one, Nellie," he said. "You caught it like a pro." Waino tossed the fish into a pail of water.

By lunch time, we'd landed four bass and three big crappies. The latter fight almost as much as bass, though you usually hook them trolling.

We rowed to the pine-needle laden shore on what had been our side, tied the boat to the dock, and took twins and food, a six-pack of beer, and a canvas tarp which Waino spread under the jack pines forming an umbrella for the sun. June beetles, probably eleators, were clicking; swifts sailed through the air scooping insects; breezes were skittering in tiny waves.

Dave had a b.m. After I wiped his bottom, I took the soiled diaper behind a tree, scraped it with a twig, then rinsed it in the lake. Of the twins, Mike seemed Waino's favorite, for when I returned he was feeding him a macaroon.

"Can you tell which is which?" I asked.

"Sure," he said. "I can't keep their names straight, but this one"—he pointed to Mike—"looks happier. His eyes seem more open. He reaches out to you with his hands." He laughed. "Of course, I've not known them too long."

After lunch we fished for another hour, catching nothing, for few game fish seem to bite when the sun is high. We were home by 2:30 p.m. Waino said he'd see me again, that we might go to a dance bar. "Sure," I said. "Cook the fish for your dad and the kids," he said.

We Waltzed the Whole Night Through

LIKE MOST such places, Delich's Tavern was far enough from Eagle River to escape city laws. The town of Lincoln, rural, had kept hands off taverns, dance halls, and resorts ever since the speakeasy days when many such joints were founded by members of the Al Capone gang or by other bootleggers. After the repeal of prohibition, these spots enjoyed free opening and closing times, and unrestricted gambling and prostitution. The more freedom, the more money tourists coughed up. And there was a need, for life in the Northwoods from Labor Day to Memorial Day, when the tourists had returned home, depended on income earned from vacations during the three-summer months.

To reach Delich's Tavern, that local institution, you parked in some Norway pines. If you planned to leave snockered, you parked close to the exit leading to Highway 45. The building, of logs set upright and chinked with plaster, dated to the twenties, and, though varnished, had a blue tinge. You entered a vestibule roofed with shingles. The interior was finished with knotty pine.

You dropped your wraps in the vestibule, and then proceeded to a long bar of pine exuding a woodsy odor blent with beer and cigarette fumes. Above the bar, over the central serving area, were a set of mounted deer heads, a family group of a twelve-point buck, an alert doe, plus a fawn. The last of these was sculpted back through its shoulders so you could see the mottling. Along the bar in both directions and on the wall opposite were trophies of prize muskellunge, bass, wall-eye, and northerns. When you caught something mountable, you didn't lose the meat: for the taxidermist used only skin and head. The realism of the results depended, obviously, on the taxidermist's skills. There were also mounted mallards in flight, and crappies, blue gills, bass, and perch. A stuffed porcupine, an otter with a trout in its mouth, a black bear cub, and a skunk rounded out the menagerie. Since the bar was narrow you either drank standing or seated on stools. No room for booths here.

At the far end of the bar, near the johns, was the entrance to the dance hall. Above, as you walked through, was a joker: a male deer missing his body from the shoulders forward; i.e., he was headless, so that only his rear portion was stuffed and mounted. The wag taxidermist had raised the animal's tail revealing the puckered anus, scrotum, and appendages. To your left, just before entering to dance, there was a decrepit pool table, an "heirloom," Sam Delich the owner claimed. He'd never junk it. Inside the pine panelled hall red-checked gingham curtains covered the windows.

In the mid-fifties, music at Delich's was seldom live, except on summer weekends with a country band. Music blared from a jukebox. Elvis Presley tunes dominated, with a spread of old country-western favorites, and some Crosby songs, including "Blue Hawaii," a perennial favorite. Roy Acuff, Roy Rogers, and weepy Kitty Wells and Patsy Cline tunes were popular.

On live music nights, the place was jammed. One regular, "Steamy" Goudge, a fortyish lumberjack proud of his balls, got smashed, then dropped his pants, relaxing his genitals in a pool table side pocket. Delich gave up trying to get him to stop, and customers threw dimes and nickels in the pocket until Goudge withdrew, retrieved his trousers, and went home, taking along his earnings.

Waino looked spiffy in a new Marine-style jacket over which he'd flattened his blue shirt collar. He had on tight jeans, washed only a couple of times. I wore the best of my two dresses, a cotton affair with a pleated skirt, where the pleats start where your butt crack begins. Like my other dress, this one was blue and its bolero jacket nicely covered my breasts. Pale blue seemed to suit my freckles.

I hadn't danced for so long I felt like a klutz and had to remind myself that I must just put myself in Waino's hands. Soon we were moving smoothly around the floor, dancing cheek to cheek. Other dancers stared, some even pointing at us, for the new modes were rock and roll, even when the tunes were country-western.

Linda Cline swung on the muscular arm of Will Eiler while her husband Chuck flopped on a bench mumbling to himself. Linda was a brunette I'd known since grade-school days. Her ideal, she used to brag, was Linda Darnell, and though times (and hair styles) had changed, she still resembled her, although six kids and much boozing had leached her complexion. Goofy Rex Castle, a lanky man in Levis and a sleeveless undershirt, wearing glasses so thick they gave him double eyeballs, awkwardly spun his new woman Gladys.

"I'm thirsty, Nellie," Waino said.

We took adjacent bar stools, and Waino kept smiling as he tapped his cigarette into a tray. Jack Dibbs joined us, offering Waino a job. "I've got ten acres of popple to cut. Pay's decent. Seven-fifty per hour. Or you can get paid by the cord."

Waino gave a non-committal smile. "I ain't doin' nothin' these days," he said.

Had I heard him right? The beer didn't seem to affect him—and he'd had three since we stopped dancing. He'd boasted he could hold more than a six-pack, so you couldn't tell when he was loaded. "Cat got your tongue?" I asked, poking his ribs.

That old saying "still water runs deep" sure applied to Waino. I, though, have always been a babbler, though usually I make an effort to give the other party equal time. For what can you discuss if you both don't talk? Sure, nobody much up here reads books, so you end up with first-person tales and jokes you've heard a hundred times. We're not what you'd call reflective people. Even when it comes to politics, local or international, you can say it all in a sentence, or why try? Our big current hassle is over Indian fishing rights. You're either for the red man or against him. You deliver your view (usually bigoted) and then get on with the usual bullshitting and drinking. And who reads a daily paper? They cost too much money.

"I should get on home, Waino." It was almost eleven. "Dad'll be sick of baby-sitting."

I got up from my stool.

"Sure." He downed a fifth beer, placing the empty bottle on a coaster.

When we were in the car, before starting the engine, he drew me into a kiss. "I like you, Nellie."

I'd been stung by Griffin, though I'd planned that polka. Was Waino different? I liked his quiet (so I thought) temper. I liked his touch. And Finns always look clean, like they don't have to bathe as much as the rest of us do. I guess it's because they come from tundras, live on reindeer, and have no sun they are so squeaky pale. Even their red hair is sexy—which was Kovisto's color, though the hair was peeling back at the temples. Nor had I any reason to feel he'd spurn my twins.

Instead of heading straight for home, Waino drove to Mud Minnow Lake.

"We can't stay long," I said.

"Stop being bossy," he said.

We parked on a knoll with a good view of Mud Minnow Lake below. Though the moon was in its final quarter, there was still enough light to dazzle the surface. Because of mosquitoes, we kept the windows up.

We began necking, and before I knew it he was playing around in my panties. "What the hell," I thought. "It feels pretty good."

I felt his erection on my leg. "Please, please," he sighed.

Though it was awkward in the front seat, we managed; while Griffin's gig took about twenty seconds, Waino's took seventy-five. He even managed some warm-up time. Still his climax, fast, again left me wondering: "What is this sex thing all about?"

Waino's mother lived north of Eagle River in a green tarpaper house. Though she might have hooked up water and electricity, she chose not to, keeping old country ways. She pumped her water from a pitcher pump, cooked on an old-fashioned wood-burning stove, used Aladdin mantle lamps, and had an out-door privy. She was barely five feet tall and wore her once blond hair (it was now a dirty gray) in a severe bun. She was almost chinless, and when she talked or smiled you saw spots of rot. One prominent tooth was little more than a snag. She greeted me fulsomely when Waino first introduced us.

"Come in, Nellie. Come in. Waino has told me about you." She pointed to a couch with an afghan and crocheted pillows. "Have some coffee? Or, you'd prefer tea?"

"Coffee's fine," I said, sitting on the couch beside Waino. "Black."

We sipped coffee with home-made short bread. To break the ice, I asked Mrs. Kovisto if she missed living in the woods.

She gave Waino a glance. "He's the reason I'm living in here close to town. He thought my being alone was risky, for my health is poor." She paused. "I know something though. I absolutely refuse to have what everybody else has—water, gas, indoor plumbing, or a telephone."

"You can take the girl out of the country," Waino laughed, "but you can't take the country out of the girl."

As we were about to leave, Waino said, "Mom, Nell and I are getting married. We might as well, we're together most of the time anyhow."

I couldn't believe it. In the car, I said: "You were joking, right? About our getting married."

"No," he said. "I'm serious. You, me, and the twins. Let's do it."

Two weeks later, in his mother's house, we married. His step-dad Turvi Millinen stood up for him, my sister Marge for me. Only our families were present, with Dad in charge of Dave and Mom of Mike. There was little fuss. I wore my blue dress for the last time until Dad's funeral in 1965. Waino bought me white carnations with a red rosebud in the center. He wore a blue serge suit. Irene and Balsam and Fish Dick were there. The Lutheran preacher married us. Within five minutes we were man and wife. I now had a husband and my sons a father. There was no honeymoon, for we had only sixty-five dollars between us. I had lost my job at the cranberry plant, and Waino was laid off from part-time work at the Eagle Waters Golf Course. We rented a crumbling house with fake brick tarpaper siding my brother Everett had built in the Sundstein where my parents lived when they married and where all of us were born. So, you see, things have a scary way of coming full circle. Everett charged us twenty dollars a month for rent.

* * *

What better way to end your story than on an up-beat note? And what better way to stop than when I'm sitting here waiting for more customers? Mid-May has been a scorcher, nearly eighty and so humid you can smell cricket sweat. Thunder-heads are wheeling over Con-over again. I can spot lightning, the scary kind; and we may get a tornado. If you are wearing glasses with metal rims, or have steel plates on your shoes, you'd better take them off.

I'm weary of talking. And you too must feel relief to come to the end. If you find a publisher (the idea scares me), don't let them put a hearse or a corpse on the cover. I need some dignity, right? I've used these woman muscles, tongue, and brain for nearly sixty years and have survived. Not too bad, right? A quaking aspen I've never been—more like a white birch, one that bends in a storm then flops back once the orioles begin their spring chirping.

Since there's no customer here yet I'll fill you in on my life after marrying Waino. The lanky, ruddy Finn marries me, and says he'll adopt my sons. I'm so anxious I can't read the signs, though they were there all along. His sister warned me. Three months after the wedding he announced he would never adopt my "bastards." I thought having kids of his own might temper him, bring him around to accepting my boys. So, for Kovisto I had a daughter, another daughter, a son, and another son. When I was pregnant with daughter two and we lived in Kenosha where Kovisto had a job winding armatures for Nash Kel-vinator, he was rammed by a drunk teenager in a Porsche and his skull was gouged by the car's door handle. After that, around the twentieth of every month, he'd go surly and beat me and the kids. The poor guy—his brain seemed to have menstrual cycles. The twins stayed with our folks while I supported Kovisto and my new batch of kids with many lousy jobs. After over six years of this, when I sought a divorce, he refused to leave, so I had him evicted. I moved my four new kids into Dad's welding shop, which had no insulation, a dirt floor, and no toilet facilities. Speaking of poverty!

Wish I could stop smoking. Wait. Here's a customer with Illinois license plates. They won't hang around long. Look through this fishing magazine while I tend to 'em. My son Gus subscribes. Everything you need to know about catching lunkers is in that issue.

Well, that was fast. I knew they'd be slumming, comparing our junk with theirs down south in Matoon or Cairo.

Now, I had other men. Wendell was a friend and that was that. We'd snuggle wearing our nighties, and just the warmth of another body was a luxury. Wendell was good to all six of my kids, cooked barbecues, drank a bit, and took us riding in his speed boat. He still lives near the town bridge. If you look close—stand over there by the garage—you'll see his new drinking partner. She just buried her husband Johnny Dabbs.

There was also Clyde S. who wore nothing but gray, had the typical wet-cement belly you find on local men, a gray mustache, and gray bags under his eyes which resembled a hound dog's eyes. We had a good thing for a month in his trailer parked beside my house. Then, without warning he produced five motherless half-grown kids for me to raise. I kicked him and his orphans out.

Fed up, lonesome, with my kids now out of the nest, I thought that since I'd failed with men, I'd try a woman. I found a pen pals column in a magazine you bought for me in that Laguna Beach lesbian bookstore, and wrote to this retired nurse in Montana. Her letters were affectionate. I might have been a high-school girl with a first sweetie. Before I knew it, she'd hopped a plane and was on my door step.

Matty, which was what she called herself (short for Matilda), was a slender person with a tiny head not much bigger than a coconut. Her lips looked pencilled on, and she had yellow eyebrows, and a way of swallowing her words so that you couldn't hear most of what she said. And she chain-smoked. Once in a while, she smiled. She vowed that all her life she'd craved women but never had one. Hell, she was even dumber than I was.

We tried sleeping together, and, since I didn't know what to do, and she didn't either, we were flops. After a couple of hours in the same bed, I climbed out and slept on the living room couch. I remained very mixed about these feelings. Sure, while most women probably have them, they scared me, and this I'll never resolve. I'd hoped that telling you my story would help.

When Matty claimed she had a pension, was in good health, and would share house expenses, I thought: if all this is true, at least we can be housemates. We hired a U-Haul, drove to Montana, and returned with her personal effects, most of which she crammed into the room I gave her; and there she stayed, coughing and hacking, chain-smoking, and solving endless jig-saw puzzles. It turned out that she had no income, had stomach cancer, and had already suffered three heart attacks. No pot of gold at the end of this rainbow. After two months, I demanded she leave.

I'd been working at a recycling center sorting old bottles according to color and crushed beer and soda pop cans. Minimum wage, and I froze my butt off, for this was winter and I had only a small pot-bellied stove to warm the cavernous warehouse. I was at work the day Miss Matty chose to climb into her old Dodge station wagon and leave. Before going, though, she arranged a surprise; she bought a gallon of Dutch Boy yellow paint, threw my clothes into my drier, dumped in the paint, and set it spinning. I came home before the stuff had baked to the inside. With lots of turp, I got most of my clothes clean and saved the drier. The sheriff said he'd arrest her. I said no, good riddance. Looking back, we did have a few good times, and she was decent to my kids and grandkids who accepted her.

Do I feel sorry for myself? Not on your life! As the old song goes I've been whacked down so much it feels like up to me. What's a woman to do? Can you conceive of a life without men, or, to say it like this, can you conceive without men? If those scientists who mess with genes and DNA can get sumac, spider pines, or crappies to produce sperm, why can't they bypass me—use the artificial stuff?

I'd still like to be a mechanic. Other women could join me, and we'd fill all the roles men fill, and better. Right now I'm trying to convince the Disabled American Veterans to rent me an old store-front where I can get all this junk out of my garage. I still see my Dad's hand in this, bless him, for behind every one of his houses he had a scrap heap. He died, as I said, in 1968. He dropped dead firing a .22 shell into the skull of a stray dog at the dump. Liz Greek and her Mom brought the dog. When Dad fell into flames, and the Greeks pulled him out, it was too late.

I was going to end with his funeral, for that would bring his influence on my life full circle. But I've changed my mind. Though he's here in the cemetery—his bones, that is—he lives within me, and in the junk I pile up against and inside my garage. So, I've ended this book by talking about him anyway.

I hope I can get that store-front. Eagle River needs a quality second-hand store. I'll upgrade my merchandise.

Bob, before you leave, I've got something for you and Paul. See that little bronze statue of a naked dude wearing an old helmet spearing a dragon? It probably held salt for some rich bugger's table, probably in Europe. It turned up at a garage sale on the other side of town